Y0-DWO-646

19931

CHICAGO PUBLIC LIBRARY
HAROLD WASHINGTON LIBRARY CENTER

R0049539931

LB
1811
.C58   Colleges of
1985   education

DATE			

THE CHICAGO PUBLIC LIBRARY
EDUCATION & PHILOSOPHY

SOCIAL SCIENCES & HISTORY DIVISION

© THE BAKER & TAYLOR CO.

COLLEGES
of
EDUCATION

THE NATIONAL SOCIETY
FOR THE STUDY OF EDUCATION

Series on Contemporary Educational Issues
Kenneth J. Rehage, Series Editor

The 1985 Titles:
Adapting Instruction to Individual Differences, Margaret C. Wang and
Herbert J. Walberg, editors
Colleges of Education: Perspectives on Their Future, Charles W. Case and
William A. Matthes, editors

The National Society for the Study of Education also publishes
Yearbooks which are distributed by the University of Chicago Press.
Inquiries regarding all publications of the Society, as well as inquiries
about membership in the Society, may be addressed to the Secretary-
Treasurer, 5835 Kimbark Avenue, Chicago, IL 60637. Membership
in the Society is open to any who are interested in promoting the
investigation and discussion of educational programs.

Committee on an Expanded Publication Program

Daniel U. Levine, Herbert J. Walberg, cochairmen

Edgar G. Epps   Robert J. Havighurst
Elizabeth H. Fennema   Harriet Talmage
              Kenneth J. Rehage, ex officio

Board of Directors of the Society—1984

Harry S. Broudy   John I. Goodlad
Margaret Early   A. Harry Passow
Elliot W. Eisner   Ralph W. Tyler
              Kenneth J. Rehage, ex officio

COLLEGES
of
EDUCATION

Perspectives on Their Future

Edited by

Charles W. Case
and
William A. Matthes

University of Iowa

McCutchan Publishing Corporation

2526 Martin Luther King Jr. Way
Berkeley, California 94704

LB
1811
.C58
1985

R0049 5 39931

Library of Congress Catalog Card Number 84–61701
ISBN 0–8211–0230–3

© 1985 by McCutchan Publishing Corporation. All rights reserved
Printed in the United States of America

Cover design by Terry Down, Berkeley, California
Typesetting composition by Vera-Reyes, Inc., Manila

Contents

PART III
Colleges of Education: New Opportunities   **187**

Contributors

Robert V. Carlson, University of Vermont
Charles W. Case, University of Iowa
Hendrik D. Gideonse, University of Cincinnati
Kenneth R. Howey, University of Minnesota — Minneapolis
David Imig, American Association of Colleges for Teacher Education
Owen Levin, Wisconsin Department of Health and Social Services
William A. Matthes, University of Iowa
Sally Mertens, Alverno College, Milwaukee, Wisconsin
Leonard Nadler, George Washington University, Washington, D.C.
John R. Palmer, University of Wisconsin — Madison
Jay D. Scribner, Temple University
Darold A. Treffert, Fond du Lac County Health Care Center, Fond du Lac, Wisconsin
Tom Weirath, Wisconsin Department of Health and Social Services, Madison, Wisconsin
Sam J. Yarger, University of Wisconsin — Milwaukee

PART I

Colleges of Education: Scope and Perspectives

INTRODUCTION

Responses to current stresses and strains on colleges of education in major universities in the United States provide the focus of this book. Yet in a larger sense, the authors, while always conscious of the present, unfetter themselves to interpret trends as well as existing pressures. Often, they are concerned with the role colleges of education can play in the evolution of the profession of education, as well as with the expanding definition of education. In this latter context, the relationship of professional educators to other human service professions is examined.

In Part I the authors deal with common themes from different perspectives. They examine the historical development of the preparation of teachers and other educators. They describe the tensions experienced by colleges of education, which are in one sense professional schools for a profession that is not quite a profession. In another sense, colleges of education are viewed as part of the liberal arts tradition. The authors note the impact these tensions have on the quality of faculty, students, and programs and on the allocation of

1

resources. There seems to be a confusion within universities as to whether a college of education and its faculty should behave as a professional school or as a liberal arts college.

In various ways the authors describe the tensions existing between faculty in colleges of education and educational practitioners, and among faculty regarding the knowledge base for designing preparation programs. There is a tug-of-war between faculty who see a "commonsense" approach to preparation and those who contend the programs should be based on the results of research and be guided by constant inquiry.

The differences in roles and functions of a college of education in providing preservice and in-service education are examined in these chapters. While greater consensus seems apparent in the case of preservice education, there is tension there also. It appears that very little consensus exists in colleges of education regarding their role in in-service education. There is lack of agreement on this point in the profession generally, as well as in state legislative bodies. Some of the authors consider the role of colleges of education in other human service professions, and, in some instances, they sharply disagree with one another. This topic is the primary focus of later chapters in this volume.

There is general agreement among the authors of chapters in Part I that if education is to continue to develop into a profession, the major research universities and their colleges of education must continue to commit their energy, expertise, and resources to this goal. As John Palmer states: "The training of teachers and other school personnel is of vital concern to this nation. Such training cannot be mediocre, and it must be conducted by the best that our system of higher education has to offer." Palmer believes that teacher preparation should be conducted in major public and private universities with their full array of liberal arts and professional preparation and their proven commitment to research and the advancement of knowledge.

In Chapter I David Imig provides an excellent overview of the demography of preparation in education. He summarizes information on the characteristics of faculty, students, and programs in the 1,340 colleges and universities in the United States that prepare educators. He takes note of projections regarding the supply of and demand for teachers. He discusses the current trends regarding admission and exit examinations, directions for changes in preparation programs,

accreditation, certification, and resources for the preparation of educators. In his concluding section he poses issues and questions that he
sees as critical for the next phase of development in professional
preparation.

The chapter by Hendrik Gideonse looks beyond the present to
provide a blueprint for the preparation of educators in the future. His
rationale for the development of teaching into a profession is based on
the concept of teaching as an intellectual activity with intellectual
ends. He sees professional preparation as having four components:
liberal education, content mastery, disciplinary underpinnings of a
profession, and knowledge associated with different professional roles.
He advocates a longer period of time for professional preparation of
educators than is presently the case.

In his discussion of teacher education, John Palmer examines its
development and status within major public universities. He describes the tensions within professional schools between those engaged in the preparation of practitioners and those involved in the
preparation of researchers, as well as the tensions between those
conducting basic research and those doing applied research. He also
notes the tensions between faculty in professional schools and practitioners. While he advocates changes to address these tensions, he
clearly opts for the importance of having major universities endure
these tensions rather than advocating their role in teacher preparation.

Jay Scribner directs attention in Chapter 4 to the evolution of
teacher preparation in urban universities, carefully relating that
evolution to urban development and change. He points to the paradoxes faced by urban universities: elitism versus egalitarianism, quality versus quantity, institutional versus individual influence, and professionalism versus humanism. He describes the characteristic responses of urban universities to social and economic conditions in the
past two decades as "managing by addition." He characterizes their
present responses as "managing by decline" and proposes that the
responses in the future should emphasize "managing change," particularly through mechanisms that make strategic planning possible.

In the final chapter of Part I Sam Yarger, Sally Mertens, and
Kenneth Howey are concerned primarily with the issues surrounding
continuing professional development and the role of colleges of education in this vital activity. They contend that the usual graduate
offerings in colleges of education do not address the continuing

professional development needs and interests of practitioners. They sharply disagree with those who argue for an expanded mission for colleges of education to include roles in human services, insisting that colleges of education should first do a better job with their natural constituencies. In their view, colleges of education do not have the capacity or the resources to engage in the continuing professional development of other professionals.

The chapters in Part I offer various perspectives on the issues and problems with which colleges of education are faced today. The authors provide a background against which possibilities for future developments in teacher education, including proposals for an expanded mission for colleges of education, may be considered. Some of these possibilities are the subjects of the chapters that follow in Part II and of the concluding chapter of this volume.

CHAPTER

1

The Scope of Teacher Education

David G. Imig

For more than six decades the federal government has invested significant resources in teacher education. These investments began in the years before World War I and continue in the present era of declining federal resources for education. They helped to build the capacity of teacher education programs in a variety of curricular areas ranging from vocational to handicapped education and from reading to mathematics education. The federal programs have taken a multiplicity of forms—from fellowships to grants for curriculum development, including support for faculty development, research and dissemination, leadership development, equipment purchases, and program design evaluation. Generally, the federal investments were categorical programs and initiated only after efforts were made to effect changes elsewhere in the educational system.[1]

While the initial efforts were designed to strengthen university-based teacher education, later investments that focused on teacher education sought to develop alternative teacher education programs. This was evident for the first time in 1965 with passage of the Elementary and Secondary Education Act, which significantly shifted federal policy toward teacher education. At that time, local education agencies were permitted to use federal monies to initiate teacher development programs. In addition, in what some consider to be the most important federal policy decision affecting schools of education, the Cooperative Research Act was amended to establish educational laboratories to develop and demonstrate educational innovations and to train teachers in their use. Finally, Teacher Corps legislation, initiated in 1965, prompted a teacher-intern model. Whereas earlier federal investments in teacher education had concentrated on building the capacity of schools of education, these three federal acts attempted to move teacher preparation, research, and development *out* of the exclusive domain of higher education.

These pieces of legislation, as well as the controversial Educational Professions Development Act of 1967 (EPDA), continued to erode the role of schools, colleges, and departments of education as the training sites for the profession. The EPDA was expected to consolidate some fifteen discretionary programs for the purposes of program administration and local coordination. Teacher renewal sites were to become a local delivery system for the in-service training of teachers. While this effort was curtailed, and the Education Amendments of 1976 (P.L. 94–482) repealed the EPDA, federal policy further encouraged site-specific training through establishment of the Teacher Centers program. By the end of 1967, the federal investment in professional preparation was substantial—over $300 million in grants, contracts, and other awards through some forty separate programs administered by the U. S. Office of Education and still more millions of dollars invested through a host of programs outside the Office of Education.[2] However, this money was shared among three groups: institutions of higher education, local education agencies, and state education agencies. Federal legislation, either by intent or benign neglect, had cast the current set of actors in teacher education.

The Education Consolidation and Improvement Act of 1981, included in the Omnibus Budget Reconciliation Act (P.L. 97–208), was the prime force in moving this debate to a new level. It also presented schools of education with unique problems because they had been the primary recipients of funds from the thirty-three categorical programs consolidated. Schools of education had developed a significant number of programs responsive to federal funding opportunities and now saw their termination as a significant disruption. The phasing-in of the block grants helped to alleviate some of the abruptness of this move but did not prevent the laying off of significant numbers of faculty and termination of graduate student fellowships.

In order to consider effective ways of enhancing the system of teacher education, we begin by describing that system. Included are predictions of likely futures for schools of education and the identification of a series of issues for consideration and action.

AN OVERVIEW OF THE STRUCTURE AND FORMS OF TEACHER EDUCATION

The task of preparing teachers for today's schools while maintaining and upgrading the knowledge and skills of practicing teachers is an enormous undertaking. As the training arm of the teaching profession, teacher education is charged with developing knowledge and skills as bases for practice, with preparing personnel for entry into the profession (preservice), and with contributing to the ongoing development of practicing professionals (in-service). The first two of these functions are integral parts of higher education. The third is shared with local staff development programs. The tasks of redefining the function and form of teacher education—both preservice and in-service—and of building a more integrated system for delivery represent challenges for the near future.

Preservice Education

Function and Form. Today, the initial or basic preparation of teachers, counselors, principals, and school administrators takes place in some 1,340 institutions of higher education. More than 70 percent of all such institutions provide teacher education programs, although the largest share of prospective teachers (45 percent) are trained in public, master's-level state colleges and universities that were at one time normal schools. A representative sample of the 1,340 higher education institutions offering education programs indicated that all offer at least one bachelor's program, 66 percent operate master's programs, 36 percent offer sixth-year programs, and 21 percent offer doctoral programs.[3]

Despite severe economic pressures confronting institutions of higher education, the enterprise is characterized by resiliency. Only a few institutions have closed or "down-sized" their education programs, while the number of institutions offering education degrees actually increased slightly during the 1970s.[4] The retention of teacher education at the University of California at Berkeley was viewed by many as an example of this resiliency.

Faculty. Although a major study of education faculty is underway at the University of Vermont, the most recent data profiling faculty were produced by Bruce Joyce and his colleagues. They reported that over 40,000 persons teach in these programs, collectively known as schools, colleges, and departments of education. Their data showed that 85 percent of faculty held doctorates, 60 percent were tenured, and more than 90 percent had a mean of eight years' experience in elementary and secondary schools.[5] Francis Fuller and Oliver Bown added that most teacher educators share humble social-class origins and low status in comparison with their academic colleagues. They more often hold paying jobs while working for a degree, enter the faculty later, perhaps with the Ed.D., and so are less likely to have acquired the scholarly credentials valued by academicians.[6]

In a later study, size of faculty varied greatly, ranging from 1 to 480 full-time equivalent members at the undergraduate level and 1 to 400 full-time equivalent members at the graduate level. This study also found a largely white, male, and campus-bound faculty (not engaging in off-campus consultancies), who placed primary emphasis on their teaching assignments.[7] Everett Ladd and Seymour Lipset found the same kind of faculty to be supportive of campus activism, black concerns, and student participation, although its self-perception was one of considerable conservatism. They also revealed that the education faculty, sometimes criticized for lack of scholarship, publishes at a rate comparable with faculty members in other disciplines.[8] The latest American Association of University Professors study reported that full professors in education, on the average, earn $5,000 less than the mean salary of colleagues in other disciplines and that they rank below all other disciplines (excluding library science and fine arts) in salary levels.[9]

Students. Schools of education span a broad range of enrollments: from 1 to 7,000 full-time equivalent students at the lower division level, from 1 to 7,100 full-time equivalent students at the upper division level, and from 2 to 3,000 full-time equivalent students at the graduate level.[10]

The most pervasive and serious problems confronting schools of education are decline in enrollment, curtailment of programs, and retrenchment of faculty. The National Center for Education Statistics (NCES) documented that enrollments in education fell from 1.1 million in 1966 to 781,000 in 1978, and the National Education Association reported that productivity decreased from an all-time high level of 317,254 in 1972 to 159,485 in 1980—a decrease of 49.7 percent.[11] The NCES projected further declines before an upturn in enrollment at the end of the decade. Parallel to the decline in the number of bachelor's degree recipients in education is the decline in the number of all bachelor's degree recipients. Bachelor's degree recipients in education represented 21 percent of all recipients in 1970–71 but declined to slightly less than 13 percent by 1979–80.[12]

The profile of students in education exhibits characteristics long associated with the public school teacher. More than two-thirds are female; almost 90 percent are white; the majority come from middle-class homes; one-third of their mothers are homemakers; 50 percent attend universities and colleges no more than fifty miles from home; and 25 percent transferred into their present program from a community or junior college.[13]

Students entering teacher preparation programs often transfer from other college majors. Their documented reasons for entering teacher education include a desire to work with young people, the opportunity for rendering an important service, and an interest in their subject fields. Extrinsic factors such as employment security, financial rewards, and status are not listed prominently as important incentives.[14]

Additional information suggests that, on the average, individuals who become teachers are less academically qualified than those who enter many other fields. Drawing upon the work of Phillip C. Schlechty and of W. Timothy Weaver, the NCES reported:

> Since 1973, college-bound seniors taking the Scholastic Aptitude Test (SAT) have been asked to choose from a list "the field that would be your first choice for your college curriculum." Data show that the SAT scores in 1973 of intended education majors were lower than those of all college-bound seniors and by 1981, the gap in test performance had widened further. The SAT verbal mean score for college-bound seniors whose first choice was education declined from 418 in 1973 to 391 in 1981, a drop of 27 points, while the SAT verbal mean score for all college-bound seniors declined from 445 to 424, a drop of 21 points. At the same time, the SAT mathematics mean score for college-bound seniors whose first choice was education declined from 449 to 418, a drop of 31 points, while the SAT mathematics mean for all college-bound seniors declined from 481 to 466, a drop of 15 points. A

comparison of scores between college-bound seniors whose first choice was education and those whose first choice was not education would yield even greater differences.[15]

It should be noted, however, that a growing number of studies based on college grades are showing that teacher education students outperform noneducation students in academic subject matter courses. Several recent studies found that, in virtually all cases, the mean grade-point average of the education majors was above that of the noneducation majors in subject matter courses *within the academic disciplines of the noneducation majors*.[16]

Job Placement. During much of the 1970s, graduates of schools of education experienced difficulty in finding jobs. A survey of 1974–75 bachelor's degree recipients in spring 1976 showed that 105,000 of 229,500 newly qualified teaching candidates were not teaching. Two years later, a survey of 1976–77 bachelor's degree recipients indicated that by spring 1978, these numbers had declined—71,000 out of 177,200 were not teaching. However, more recent NCES data indicate that 1976–77 bachelor's recipients newly qualified to teach fared much beter in the labor market than did liberal arts graduates.[17]

In spring 1983, while school districts in certain parts of the country were laying off teachers, others were reporting unfilled vacancies. This anomaly is apparently due to different growth patterns in different states, regions, and localities. While the "sunbelt" experiences significant teacher shortages, many areas in the "frostbelt" continue to lay off teachers. Selected states are reporting "great difficulty in filling positions" in certain assignment areas, while these and other states are indicating "general employment of persons with substandard qualifications." In spring 1980, thirty states were reporting "great difficulty" in finding mathematics teachers, thirty-two in finding special education teachers for the secondary level and twenty-seven for the elementary level, eighteen for teachers of physical sciences and agriculture, and twenty-seven for teachers of industrial arts. Thus, a shortage is evident in many parts of the country and is likely to grow significantly in the coming decade.[18]

Although there is great uncertainty about the potential impact of the "reserve pool" of trained but unplaced teachers and former teachers on any potential shortage, the NCES has estimated that by 1985 the supply of new teachers will fall short of demand by 14.9

percent—with even greater shortages likely in the late 1980s.[19] While subsequent NCES projections reversed these estimates and projected a supply of new teacher graduates approximately equal to the demand for additional teachers, these projections appear to ignore a commonly overlooked fact that during the 1980s the number of members in the 18- to 21-year-old cohort, from which prospective teachers are drawn, will decrease by over 2.6 million persons, a decline of 15 percent. This will force schools of education to compete for potential applicants with other programs in the university, with the military, and with the job market. This comes at a time when student preferences for teacher education have fallen significantly and continue to fall; less than 5 percent of the 1981 freshman class indicated a preference for teacher education, down almost 30 percent from a decade earlier.[20] Indications are that this trend is likely to continue.

While supply is affecting this situation, shifting enrollment trends at the elementary and secondary levels exacerbate conditions. In public elementary schools, enrollment peaked in 1971 at 27.7 million. An enrollment of 24.2 million was reported for fall 1979; a further drop to 23.6 million occurred in 1983. From now on, enrollment may begin to rise slightly again. The U.S. Census Bureau has projected that the total population of 5- to 13-year-olds will rise from a low of 29.1 million in 1985 to 32.6 million in 1990. Should the birth rate rise, enrollment could be substantially higher.[21]

Although the future pattern of elementary school enrollment presents a mixed picture, that for secondary education is much clearer. The Census Bureau projects that the number of 14- to 17-year-olds will fall from 15.8 million in 1980 to 14.4 million in 1985 and to 12.8 million by 1990. Only in 1991 will a slight increase begin. Thus, high school enrollment can be expected to fall throughout the 1980s. Of course, not all of these 14- to 17-year-olds are in school. The NCES reports that enrollment in grades 9 through 12 in public schools peaked in 1976 at 14.3 million. It is projected to fall to 12.7 million by 1981, continuing down to 11.8 million in 1986.[22] As a result, the job possibilities for new high school teachers seem quite bleak, and high school administrators can expect to face the multiple personnel, curriculum, and budget problems associated with declining enrollments throughout the decade.

Compounding the shortage problem is the growing use of admission and exit examinations that has resulted in a significant decline in the number of minority applicants for teaching positions. For example, Florida, one of the first states to develop its own teacher certification examination, is experiencing an 80 percent passing rate for all college graduates taking its state-developed tests. However, black students are failing at a rate of nearly 70 percent, while white students are failing at less than a 15 percent rate. Florida certified about 5,500 new teachers in 1981; about 200 were black. Louisiana, one of several southern states using the National Teacher Examination for certification, provides another example. Although its overall passage rate is about 70 percent, the percentage of black graduates certified has been in the 10 to 20 percent range.[23] Louisiana certified 2,800 teachers in 1981; the two largest predominantly black institutions produced fewer than forty of these.

A number of black teacher educators, noting the potential impact of this phenomenon on staffing patterns for urban schools, warns that the very existence of the black public school teacher is threatened.[24] The increasing minority population, as a percentage of the total population, and the growth of ethnic diversity require that schools be able to respond to a wider range of interests, needs, and backgrounds. During the coming decade significant recruitment efforts must be mounted among non-Anglo racial and ethnic groups if the teaching force is to remain representative of the larger society.

Program Profile.   Typically, a teacher preparation program includes four components: a solid foundation in general education or liberal studies, including basic skills; advanced study in one or more academic subjects; professional studies in generic teaching domains, foundational studies, and specialized pedagogical study; and a practicum or student teaching experience.

In fulfilling the requirements of the first two components, education students may devote from 67 to 75 percent of total course work hours outside the school of education, depending on whether they are preparing to teach in an elementary or secondary school. Students preparing to teach in an elementary school devote 41 percent of their program to professional study; only 30 percent of a secondary program goes to professional study.[25] In professional courses, students practice a broad repertoire of teaching skills and learn to work successfully with parents, peers, and supervisors.

At present, a number of efforts are underway to alter the structure and form of preservice teacher education. Recurrent allegations of needless content duplication and watered-down courses have been met by efforts to use systems planning and technology to alleviate duplication, to use research findings, and to incorporate clinical experiences. Working contrary to this approach, however, is

> the ever-lengthening list of curricular accretions in schools, brought on by various societal ills: sexism, racism, economic inequality, illiteracy, domestic instability, unemployment, injustice, urban unrest, social disorder and lawlessness, drug abuse, crime, juvenile delinquency, sexual permissiveness, litigiousness, corruption, and so on *ad infinitum*—all of which likewise impact upon teacher education.[26]

Meeting these demands by adding content to an already overburdened curriculum has been a continuing problem for schools of education. Sacrificing general education to accommodate these demands is unacceptable. Restructuring and realigning existing programs are appropriate responses.

Extended Programs. A promising response to the time constraints on teacher training is to extend initial preparatory programs to five or more years. Such a change would accommodate the greater array of research findings and new knowledge, as well as respond to the clamor of external agencies for the addition of responsibilities. The inadequacy of a four-year bachelor's program for teaching pedagogy is one of the major problems confronting teacher education. While there has been in the last thirty years an explosion of knowledge in areas of teaching and learning, there has been a corresponding decline in the amount of time allotted to preparing teachers to use that knowledge. Comparing the growth and decline of quarter hours of student preparation for careers in teaching, law, pharmacy, and civil engineering at the University of Florida over the past fifty years, David Smith and Sue Street found that while other programs increased the time for professional study during the past thirty years, there had been a decline in the number of quarter hours available for teacher education.[27] Extended programs for initial preparation seem to offer one response to the limits on "life space." Such plans have already been put into place at schools such as Austin College in Texas, the University of Florida, the University of New Hampshire, the University of Kansas, and North Texas State University. Despite the fact that such programs are more demanding, enrollments in them have grown.

Resources. Funding for teacher education is another major concern. Bruce Peseau and Paul Orr concluded in one phase of an ongoing study that more is spent per year educating a typical third-grader ($1,400) than training a teacher ($927). At the same time, according to these researchers, the average annual expenditure by each full-time equivalent college or university student is $2,363. The fact is that teacher education is revenue-producing, which explains in part why it is offered by so many institutions of higher education. As recently as 1977, teacher education generated 11 percent of all university student-credit-hour production but, in return, received less than 3 percent of the institution's programmatic resources.[28]

The use of a weighted student-credit-hour measure as the quantitative determinant for the distribution of resources within universities is a major source of concern, particularly when schools of education are expected to conduct an extensive array of outreach or service programs for school districts. Such activities typically do not generate credit hours and, therefore, do not qualify for university allocations. Some states have recognized this constraint and have freed certain percentages of funds for schools of education to conduct workshops, seminars, or assessment activities for local education agencies.

Responsiveness to Preservice Conditions. Given these overviews, the anticipated teacher shortage, and the apparent diminished quality of the applicant pool, several likely futures for schools of education can be projected.*

1. The current preoccupation with issues of quality will lead to programs that are more rigorous and challenging in both general and professional education.

2. The significant demographic and ethnic shifts our society is experiencing will place new emphasis upon foundational studies in education, that is, on the premises and assumptions of schooling in a democratic, pluralistic society. Issues of transitional bilingualism and cultural pluralism will receive renewed attention along with elements of global awareness.

---

*Many of these scenarios are drawn from a series of papers commissioned by the Educational Testing Service on the future of the National Teacher Examination. Among the contributors to this series were George Denemark, Kenneth Howey, and Richard Wisniewski.

3. Rigorous and explicit provisions for the recruitment into teaching of talented members of ethnic minorities will be effected.

4. The emphasis upon integration of experiences and course work in initial preparation programs—culminating in competency examinations—will lead to the setting of goals and objectives that extend beyond individual faculty judgments and instead represent broad institutional agreements on teacher preparation, ending (it is to be hoped) the proliferation of missions and fragmentation of roles that characterize many schools of education.

5. The integration of theory and practice will also lead to renewed emphasis upon "clinical pedagogy," "early entry experiences," and "internships," paralleling the recommendations of B. O. Smith's *A Design for a School of Pedagogy* (1980).

6. Teacher education will assume greater responsibility for initial entry or beginning teacher programs, including supervision, assessment, and assistance.

7. The magnitude of attention by "significant publics" and their call for the use of standardized achievement tests as the primary criteria for both entrance and exit will cause the majority of preparation programs to become more standardized in terms of focus, program, and structure.

8. Enlargement of the "life space" provided for initial teacher preparation will occur, slowly, with the gradual appearance of more extended programs and master's degree programs, as the constraints and responsibilities of teacher education gain recognition.

9. There will be greater reliance upon the knowledge base as preservice students become more familiar with the following domains: (1) *diagnosis and evaluation of learning* (that is, collection of information about students to ascertain needs and problems, the ability to undertake formative and summative evaluation); (2) *planning and decision making* (that is, knowledge of proactive teaching—for example, manipulation of data and information, such as interpreting standardized test scores, responding to recommendations of school psychologists, and developing courses to sequence actions); (3)*management of student conduct* (that is, classroom management and organization); (4) *contextual or ecological variables* (that is, an understanding of variables that affect student learning and

development); (5) *management of instruction* (that is, interactive teacher behavior, including a thorough knowledge of different instructional approaches and the use of existing and emerging media); and (6) *teacher evaluation and professional responsibilities* (that is, self-assessment and improvement, understanding of responsibilities regarding the profession and the community, interpersonal skills).[29]

10. New emphasis upon technological literacy will generate a demand for teachers who possess minimal competence in the use of computers and other technology and will lead to critical concerns about equity among schools of education, with the "have and have not" issue gaining importance.

In-service Professional Development

In-service, staff, or professional development and/or continuing education as they presently exist in the United States represent an enormously complex but undocumented system affecting the nation's 3.6 million teachers and other school personnel and employing as many as a quarter of a million staff development personnel at a cost of millions of dollars. Roy Edelfeldt has described it as a system that is rooted in advanced collegiate preparation through both residential and extension programs of colleges and universities, but also as one that has witnessed the creation of a whole set of new institutions to provide in-service education and/or staff development opportunities.[30] These new organizations range from intermediate service centers and local district teacher centers to state deparment leadership academies and staff development programs.

Local education agencies now provide for "in-service days," "workshops" before the beginning and/or after the conclusion of the school year, and "special conferences" to introduce modified or new curricula. Colleges offer master's degree programs to attract teachers to graduate study. Teacher centers offer district-sponsored credits for participation, independent study, and travel. What Sam Yarger, Kenneth Howey, and others have pointed to are the important distinctions that have emerged between these programs, with local district programs emphasizing how faculty members relate to and learn from each other and how mutual stimulation for growth can develop when professionals work together.[31] College programs have responded by offering more varied academic courses; however, many

institutions have allowed their master's degree programs to deteri-
orate. According to a recent British observation: "Courses are often
fragmented and understaffed . . . in some places, little proof of work is
needed; no attempt is made to impose a coherent pattern upon it."[32]
This is at least one of the reasons that projections for earned master's
degrees suggest reductions of 30 percent during the coming decade.
There are significant efforts to concentrate on upgrading these courses.

The knowledge explosion suggests that we will need to find ways to
provide new and better forms of in-service education. The economic
conditions of the country suggest that there will be severe limitations
on the availability of resources to accomplish this goal. Incentives
must be found to stimulate collegiate programs to respond better to
teacher needs, while other incentives are necessary as motivators for
teachers to participate in these programs. Ways of aiding the staff
trainers, of improving the process used to deliver knowledge, and of
enhancing the substance and content of the presentation need serious
examination.

Accreditation, Certification, and Evaluation

National Accreditation. Accreditation is a process self-imposed by
educational institutions to ensure quality control. Two basic kinds of
accreditation are practiced: one that considers the institution as a
whole, another that examines specific programs. Current accreditation procedures for teacher education are program-specific, although
proposals for the transformation of the present system to institution or
"unit" accreditation have been made.

Fewer than half (537) of the 1,340 higher education institutions
currently have programs accredited by the National Council for
Accreditation of Teacher Education (NCATE). The NCATE represents colleges and universities, classroom teachers, and others
through thirteen stakeholder organizations and associations. While
accreditation by the NCATE is not mandatory, an increasing number
of colleges and universities are seeking this national accrediting
body's stamp of approval. The efforts currently underway to refocus
NCATE aim at strengthening its ability to identify both inadequate
and high-quality programs, streamline its procedures, and reduce
costs.

Certification and Evaluation. All fifty states have procedures for the
issuance of teaching certificates to individuals who complete a set of

prescribed minimum requirements. These procedures date back to 1825 when the Ohio legislature authorized county school superintendents to examine candidates and issue certificates for teaching. Today, all states have centralized teacher certification in their state education agencies, and with few exceptions, the completion of an "approved" college or university program in teacher education serves as the basis for certification.[33] Approval of teacher education programs takes place through the accreditation procedures of the NCATE or the National Association of State Directors of Teacher Education and Certification. Certification is currently undergoing a number of profound changes:

1. *Proliferation of Certificates.* There has been a tremendous proliferation of certificates classified by "type" (teacher, administrator, counselor, and so forth), "field" (specialization of teaching field), and "level" (nursery school, kindergarten, middle school, and so forth). Georgia currently issues certificates in eight fields, Louisiana has certificates for eight types of school personnel, and a number of states recognize five distinct school levels.

   Currently there is significant debate regarding the desire by some to move toward more comprehensive certificates, while others—exhibiting considerable distrust of local superintendents and principals with regard to improper assignments—want to retain, if not enlarge upon, the types, levels, and fields certified. Those seeking reforms in certification will probably have to wait until there are basic curriculum and structural reforms in elementary and secondary schools.

2. *Use of Tests in Initial Certification.* Another concern is the use of standardized tests as integral parts of the certification process. Certification by examination was common as recently as the 1930s when it was gradually replaced by graduation from normal school or college. Today we see a significant reintroduction of competency-based teacher certification. In 1981 ten states had provisions in effect, and by 1982 three more were expected to begin. More than half of these had their own state-developed examination, all but one of the rest used the National Teacher Examination, and one state, South Carolina, used both NTE and a state-developed examination.[34]

3. *Emergency Certification.* The pressures of staff availability, schedul-

ing, and funding are causing local education systems to assign teachers to specialized courses for which they are not prepared. All states have provisions for the issuance of interim, provisional, temporary, and emergency certificates. The National Institute of Education and the National Center for Education Statistics, in cooperation with the American Association of Colleges of Teacher Education, are attempting to ascertain the numbers of teachers awarded "nonstandard" certificates allowing them to teach out of their field. Reports from many parts of the country of improper assignments number in the thousands, and the potential teacher shortage is likely to exacerbate this problem. Information systems in many states lack data on the practice of issuing special certificates for persons who do not meet the regular requirements.

Parallel to this phenomenon is the waiving of existing certification regulations to enable local systems to employ arts and science graduates to teach subjects for which qualified teachers are unavailable. The Southern Regional Education Board (SREB) has advocated the modification of certification regulations to permit the use of graduates in mathematics and science "who lack professional education preparation" and of "out-of-field" assignments for teachers in "surplus fields."[35] The state of Virginia has recently implemented the SREB recommendations and moved to permit liberal arts graduates to receive provisional certification.[36]

4. *Performance Assessment Prior to Regular Certification.* Other aspects of the current debate on certification center on: (1) delaying initial certification for one year (Florida, Oklahoma, and Maryland), two years (Virginia), or three years (California and New York), during which period the candidate satisfies peers, mentors, principals, and/or college supervisors of his or her teaching competence while teaching a reduced load; and (2) modifying or eliminating permanent or "lifelong certification" by requiring more frequent renewal, additional semester hours of graduate work or professional development units within specified periods of time, and use of evaluations of teacher performance. Experimentation with both of these aspects of certification is likely to increase in the coming years.

Currently there are many different points of view about accreditation and certification represented among groups and individuals at the state and national levels. Often the positions taken are reminiscent of those held in earlier decades, for example, positions based on the belief that all one needs in order to teach is a thorough grasp of the subject to be taught. Others envision professional preparation taking a form and structure that parallels the preparation received in fields such as law and medicine.

QUESTIONS FOR CONSIDERATION AND ACTION*

The above description of the function, form, and structure of the preparation of professional educators leads to issues and questions that should be examined if the profession is to advance to its next stage of development.

Issues for Action

Among the host of issues confronting professional education during the forthcoming decade will be those emerging from efforts to do the following:

1. Reduce the number of schools, colleges, and departments of education offering teacher education and find ways to link institutions with various emerging roles and missions. To effect this, professional school models must be examined, information gathered and analyzed, and the results disseminated.

2. Recruit and retain a diversified and high-quality faculty in pedagogy at both basic and academic levels within the university and in staff development training positions. To effect this, faculty and staff must be provided with development opportunities including the option of returning to the elementary and secondary classroom; reward and tenure systems must be developed that accommodate the needs of the profession as a whole instead of just the academy. Inexpensive and reliable information systems must be counted upon to provide significant staff development opportunities.

---

*The author owes a debt of gratitude to Marilyn Rauth of the American Federation of Teachers who assisted in formulating an initial set of these issue questions.

3. Enhance the quality and quantity of the applicant pool, giving serious attention to the recruitment of talented women and members of minorities. To effect this, the public image must be changed regarding the role and importance of the teacher and teacher education, and appropriate ways of assessing and evaluating beginning teachers must be found. Tremendous information needs are inherent in these efforts.

4. Develop professionally sound ways of addressing teacher shortages in numerous fields. To effect this, new staffing patterns for schools, new incentives for teachers, and new technologies for delivery must be explored.

5. Build more rigorous and realistic preparation programs that draw upon the expanding knowledge base and give renewed attention to bilingual and multicultural issues and global awareness.

6. Experiment with various structural reforms that provide for extended programs in teacher education, facilitate the entry of beginning teachers into school environments, integrate theory and practice, and rely upon more and earlier clinical experiences.

7. Examine the appropriateness of a national curriculum for teacher education based on student competence and strengthened assessment procedures. To effect this, programs, goals, and objectives must be constructed to extend beyond individual faculty judgments to represent broad institutionwide agreements on teacher preparation.

8. Place greater emphasis on technological literacy for the beginning teacher.

9. Analyze and structure in-service needs of teachers, continue to enhance delivery systems, and effect additional in-service incentives for practicing teachers.[37]

Questions for Consideration

The information I have presented describes the function and form of teacher education. To facilitate discussion of the information, the following questions deserve the attention of both public policymakers and education professionals.

Function and Form of Teacher Education. The specificity of purpose, the focus on the clientele, and the appropriateness of the design of teacher education as it is currently formed and performed by educational institutions suggest the following questions.

1. How can we improve the quality of teacher education candidates? What changes are needed in recruitment, selection, admission, and retention for teacher education? What types of incentives could be used to attract stronger candidates? Should testing for admission into teacher education programs be used? Which tests should be used? By whom should they be administered?

2. How do we attract a richer mix of academically able women and minority group members into teacher education programs?

3. What criteria should be used to judge candidates for admission? What combination of tests, grade-point averages, experience, interviews, and recommendations should be used? What do studies on beginning teachers tell us about teacher candidates?

4. How should supply-demand data be used to affect recruitment and counseling of preservice candidates? How do we deal with the present teacher shortages in science and mathematics?

5. Given the use of formula funding (often based on a weighted complexity factor) for programs in schools of education, what incentives can be provided that will stimulate efforts to raise the admission standards without "driving down" enrollments and thereby reducing resources? What incentives can be found to enable schools of education to undertake noncredit, off-campus, technical assistance and in-service work? Should the faculty of schools of education be part of existing promotion tenure and reward systems, or should alternative systems be established? How do we attract and infuse quality into heavily tenured institutions experiencing significant curtailments?

6. Does government, both state and federal, have a special financial role to play in the preparation of personnel for the education professions as contrasted to other professional fields? What are the minimum levels of support needed to assure quality of preservice education? What should be the role of the states in providing financial support for teacher education apart from their support of higher education? Do local school districts, because they are

the beneficiaries of teacher education programs, have a responsibility to share in the cost of teacher education?

7. What responsibilities should the K–12 community assume relative to fostering a better climate for teacher education on the campus? What types of new, collaborative arrangements must be established to promote "ownership" by the K–12 community in teacher education? Does a redesigned National Council for Accreditation of Teacher Education offer a means to achieve part of this ownership?

8. What changes are needed in the content, sequence, and length of the teacher education program to accommodate the expanding knowledge base, the demands of computerization, and other technological breakthroughs and the need for field-oriented, clinical, or laboratory components in teacher education? What priority should be given to these possibilities? What attention should be given to extended programs?

9. What alterations need to take place in the general education component provided for prospective teachers and in academic specialization studies? Should both elementary and secondary precertification programs require an academic specialization? Should changes in emphasis be given to educational psychology vis-à-vis other social and behavioral sciences that are part of preprofessional study in education?

10. How do we overcome the fragmentation that characterizes much of teacher education? How do we gain coherence in ideologies, technologies, and processes? Should we go back and reassess competency-based teacher education as a systematic way of addressing this problem? Does computer-assisted instruction offer a refinement of this approach or another alternative?

11. Should teachers, administrators, and others be partners in the on-campus decision making regarding the structure and form of teacher education programs? Should all university teacher education councils include public school personnel?

12. Given the issue of status and the limitations of resources and time, can the university prepare teachers or should we create, à la David Clark and B. O. Smith, new structures between the university and the public school?

13. What impact will current efforts by schools of education to focus on human services or diversified settings have on programs of teacher education? Should they broaden their training functions to prepare persons for nonschool settings? What are the ramifications of such changes?

14. What responsibilities do schools of education have to public schools in generating interest in the career of teaching, introducing new ideas and technology to schools, keeping teachers up-to-date on skills and research findings, and helping improve and evaluate the quality of school programs?

15. How can an integrated, coordinated system of teacher education be built, one that combines the efforts of universities, schools, and professional organizations? How do we avoid competition among these entities? How do we stimulate schools of education to provide expertise and the benefits of experience to the other units?

16. Given all the groups interested in teacher education, is it possible we are moving to a single, monolithic model for teacher preparation? How much diversity can the system tolerate?

17. Given the many roles of today's schools, how should schools of education identify the goals of education they will emphasize? For example, should there be a division of responsibility between preservice professional development and staff development with respect to the roles of schools of education? At the latter end of this continuum, should the primary client group of such schools and colleges be the staffs of the staff development programs?

Staff Development. In-service, staff development, and training, as experienced (or not experienced) by teachers, ultimately by school children and, one hopes, by other educators in their own professional and personal contexts, suggest additional questions.

1. What form of evaluation system would retain the nonthreatening atmosphere needed for professional growth experiences while maintaining legitimate accountability for such programs? How can the faculty development programs of schools of education be integrated into general staff development efforts?

2. How should staff development and training needs be assessed and by whom? How do we balance the diverse preferences among teachers within a context of scarce resources? Does job-related

training take preference over individual development? Who decides?

3. What collaborative mechanisms are necessary to establish ongoing, school-based staff development and training programs? What should be the scope of such programs? Who bears the financial responsibility? What roles should principals, teachers, and policymakers play in defining needs?

4. What mechanisms are necessary to enable teachers and teacher educators to share ideas and become more involved both in and with educational research? How do we define and ensure rigor in preservice and in-service teacher education programs?

5. Will improved staff development programs require changes in staffing patterns and practices?

Certification and Evaluation. Program approval, accreditation, certification, and the evaluation (and recertification) of teachers, as well as issues related to teacher performance and the efficacy of staff development programs, provide more questions for examination.

1. If educators are to control their profession to make teaching a worthy title, what mechanisms and legal authority would enable them to guarantee quality? What roles and responsibilities should professional standards boards have? What types of assessment and evaluation procedures should be used? When should they be applied?

2. When should licensing and certification occur? Should they be separated?

3. How can meaningful accountability be built into the accreditation process? How can the costs of the present system be reduced? How can the present standards be refined? How can the costly overlap between accreditation and program approval be reduced?

4. Would rigorous beginning teacher preparation programs, including internships or initial-year programs, coupled with effective evaluation procedures, eliminate the need for expensive recertification programs? Should tenure laws be revamped?

5. Should efforts be made to reduce significantly (or eliminate) emergency, temporary, or provisional certification of teachers, particularly in an era of shortage?

Societal Inequities as a Mission of Teacher Education.   The social missions of teacher education and staff development, particularly to reduce inequities, to respond to minority cultures, and to improve the educational opportunities of children from low-income communities, provide an important area for examination.

1. How can adequate minority representation be assured in the teaching force? How can adequate numbers of handicapped persons be included in the teaching profession?

2. What can schools of education do to improve educator's skills in remediation and motivation?

3. Should all teacher education programs include substantive course work on student diversity in the classroom, for example, the gifted, the disabled, the culturally different, and so forth?

4. Since educational research documents the importance of the relationship between teacher expectations and student achievement, informs us that various instructional strategies produce different outcomes with different types of students, and outlines effective classroom management practices, are we not denying equal opportunity by failing to assure that this information is translated and accessible to teacher educators and teachers? How do we ensure incorporation of this knowledge into preservice and inservice courses?

Public Support and the Improvement of the Community.   The support or lack of support of teacher education and staff development programs by states, professional groups, and the public raises the following questions.

1. How can the public be made aware of the importance of quality education of teacher education and staff development programs?

2. If schools at all levels are to serve the public interest adequately, how can the community enter into the discussions of goals and be kept informed of progress made in meeting them? How can parents and the public become informed regarding the complexity of the teaching practice?

3. What are appropriate roles of the community in educational decision making? What is the appropriate intersection in school

matters between the public's right to participate and the professional's obligation to practice?

4. Should the teacher education curriculum include training in how to work with parents, including how to help them help their children learn and how to involve the community in the schools? If so, to what extent?

Developing a Supportive Professional Climate. Reforms in staff development programs and teacher education could provide greater satisfaction, status, and recognition of teachers by dealing with the following questions.

1. What changes in staffing patterns and reward systems are needed to prevent teaching from being a "dead-end" career? Where does differentiated staffing fit? Is this an old solution never tried or one tried and found wanting?

2. What arrangements will help break down barriers among teachers, administrators, and teacher educators, allowing them to work in a more collegial atmosphere?

This chapter has provided a profile of the form and function of the existing preparation process of education professionals in the United States. By examining this description and current debates, a number of questions have been suggested. It would seem that these questions, as well as others, must be addressed in order for the profession of education to make its next major advance. Critical inquiry, dialogue, and decisions within the profession and between the profession and its many constituencies are essential to this process. The alternatives—retreat from a professional development process, chaos, stagnation, or becoming less than a craft—are intolerable. Can this nation or its children afford such consequences?

NOTES

1. C. Emily Feistritzer and David G. Imig, "Federal Involvement in Educational Personnel Development," in *Policy for the Education of Educators: Issues and Implications,* edited by Georgianna Appignani (Washington, D.C.: American Association of Colleges for Teacher Education, 1981), pp. 90–102.

2. C. Emily Feistritzer, *Analysis of U.S. Office of Education Discretionary Programs*

Having a Professional Development of Educational Personnel Component (Washington, D.C.: U.S. Office of Education, May 1978), p. 70.

3. James Heald, *Report to the Profession, 1982* (Washington, D.C.: American Association of Colleges for Teacher Education, 1982), pp. 10–13.

4. Valena White Plisko, ed., *The Condition of Education, 1983 Edition* (Washington, D.C.: National Center for Education Statistics, 1983), pp. 174–75.

5. Bruce R. Joyce et al., *Preservice Teacher Education* (Palo Alto: Center for Educational Research at Stanford, 1977), pp. 23–28.

6. Francis F. Fuller and Oliver H. Bown, "Becoming a Teacher," in *Teacher Education*, edited by Kevin Ryan, Seventy-Fourth Yearbook of the National Society for the Study of Education, pt. 2 (Chicago: University of Chicago Press, 1975), pp. 29–30.

7. Heald, *Report to the Profession, 1982*, pp. 5–6.

8. Everett Ladd and Seymour Lipset, *The Divided Academy* (New York: McGraw-Hill, 1975), pp. 342–69.

9. Lee W. Hansen, "Surprises and Uncertainties: Annual Report on the Economic Status of the Profession, 1981–82," *Academe* 68 (July-August 1982): 3–11.

10. Heald, *Report to the Profession, 1982*, pp. 1–5.

11. Nancy B. Dearman and Valena White Plisko, *The Condition of Education, 1982 Edition* (Washington, D.C.: National Center for Education Statistics, 1982), pp. 3–4; and William S. Graybeal, *Teacher Supply and Demand in Public Schools, 1980–81* (Washington, D.C.: National Education Association, 1981), p. 5.

12. Plisko, *Condition of Education, 1983*, p. 178.

13. Joyce, *Preservice Teacher Education*, pp. 43–50.

14. Eveleen Lorton et al., *The Teachers World* (Washington, D.C.: ERIC Clearinghouse on Teacher Education, 1979), pp. 4–5.

15. Dearman and Plisko, *Condition of Education, 1982*, p. 88. See also, Phillip C. Schlechty and Victor S. Nance, "Do Academically Able Teachers Leave Education? The North Carolina Case," *Phi Delta Kappan* 63 (October 1981): 106–112, and W. Timothy Weaver, "In Search of Quality: The Need for Talent in Teaching," *Phi Delta Kappan* 61 (September 1979): 29–32, 46.

16. Michael J. Stolee, *Quality of School of Education Students and Graduates* (Milwaukee: School of Education, University of Wisconsin, Milwaukee, 1982), pp. 1–3.

17. A. Stafford Metz and Jane L. Crane, *New Teachers in the Job Market* (Washington, D.C.: National Center for Education Statistics, August 1980), p. vi.

18. Dearman and Plisko, *Condition of Education, 1982*, pp. 85–86.

19. Ibid.

20. Plisko, *Condition of Education, 1983*, p. 22; Alexander W. Astin et al., *The American Freshman: National Norms for Fall 1982* (Washington, D.C.: American Council on Education, 1982), p. 160.

21. Dearman and Plisko, *Condition of Education, 1982*, pp. 85–86.

22. Martin M. Frankel and Debra E. Gerald, *Projections of Education Statistics to 1990–91* (Washington, D.C.: National Center for Education Statistics, 1982), pp. 20–21.

23. Eva Galambos, *Preparing Blacks for the Teaching Force* (Atlanta: Southern Regional Education Board, June 29, 1982), pp. 1–3.

24. Elaine Witty, *Prospects for Black Teachers: Preparation, Certification, Employment* (Washington, D.C.: ERIC Clearinghouse on Teacher Education, 1982), pp. 19–23.

25. Dean C. Corrigan et al., *Teacher Education: Problems and Prospects* (Statement of American Association of Colleges of Teacher Education before the House Subcommittee on Postsecondary Education, September 9, 1981), p. 6.

26. Christopher J. Lucas, "The Mandate for Equity in Education: Another Challenge for Foundational Teacher Preparation," in *Foundations of Teacher Preparation: Responses to P.L. 94–142* (Minneapolis: National Support Systems Project, 1982), p. 7.

27. David C. Smith and Sue Street, "The Professional Component in Selected Professions," *Phi Delta Kappan* 62 (October 1980): 103–7.

28. Bruce Peseau and Paul Orr, "The Outrageous Underfunding of Teacher Education," *Phi Delta Kappan* 62 (October 1980): 100–102.

29. See Dale Scannell et al., *Educating a Profession: Profile of a Beginning Teacher* (Washington, D.C.: American Association of Colleges of Teacher Education, 1983), pp. 1–23.

30. Roy A. Edelfeldt, "The School of Education and In-service Education," *Journal of Teacher Education* 28 (March–April 1977): 10–14.

31. Sam J. Yarger and Gary R. Galluzzo, "Toward Solving the Dilemmas of Research on In-service Teacher Education," in *The Education of Teachers: A Look Ahead*, edited by Kenneth R. Howey and William E. Gardner (New York: Longman, 1983), pp. 169–73.

32. Harry Judge, *American Graduate Schools of Education: A View from Abroad* (New York: Ford Foundation, 1982), pp. 42–43.

33. Robert N. Bush and Peter Enemark, "Control and Responsibility in Teacher Education," *Teacher Education*, pp. 279–87.

34. J. T. Sandefur, "Teacher Competency Assessment Plans 'Little Short of Phenomenal,' " *AACTE Briefs* 3 (November 1982): 8–9.

35. Eva Galambos et al., *The Need for Quality: A Report to the SREB by Its Task Force on Higher Education in the Schools* (Atlanta: Southern Regional Education Board, 1981), pp. 11–13.

36. Zoe Ingalls, "Virginia Adopts Flexible Plan for Certifying Teachers," *Chronicle of Higher Education* 7 (July 1983): 3.

37. See Donna H. Kerr, "Teaching Competence and Teacher Education in the United States," in *Handbook of Teaching and Policy*, edited by Lee S. Shulman and Gary Sykes (New York: Longman, 1983), pp. 126–49.

CHAPTER

2

The Necessary Revolution in Teacher Education

Hendrik D. Gideonse

I am convinced that the structure of teacher education must change. I am convinced that the structure of schooling must change. I am convinced that the first steps must be taken now so that by the time my generation retires, schools and the professional education programs that prepare personnel to staff them will be recognizably and irrevocably upon a proper course.

My convictions about this revolution rest on two essential premises. The first concerns what we know about teaching and learning. From our knowledge we can define and design the optimal role of the teacher. The second essential premise relates to our image of the school. Put as simply as possible, the teaching role cannot be conceptualized apart from explicit consideration of the structure of the settings in which teaching takes place.

THE KNOWLEDGE BASE UNDERPINNING THE PROFESSION

Teaching is an intellectual activity with intellectual ends. Whatever else society demands of schooling—for example, entry-level training to the widest conceivable range of occupational choices—the purpose of education in a free society is and must remain the maintenance of the republic and those conditions that support liberal democracy. One of the most elementary preconditions is the development of sufficient intellectual understanding of the principles of our society and the manner in which it is governed. Teachers, therefore, must model intellectual attainment daily and in literally hundreds of ways.

In addition to being an intellectual task, however, teaching is also a profoundly moral activity. It involves value choices by adults for individual children and society on an ongoing basis in a particular culture at a given time. Teachers of all kinds and at all levels must be fully conversant with the complexity and responsibility of their task.

Given these two frames of reference, the knowledge base underpinning the profession has four essential components. The first is its commitment to a sound liberal education. The second dimension is mastery of the content area to be taught. Given the context and character of teaching as a profession, the third component of the knowledge base is a thorough exposure to those domains of knowledge and inquiry, broadly defined, that inform us about the nature of humanity, society, and culture. Fourth, the great and growing body of professional knowledge—knowledge pertaining to techniques, practices, characteristics of learners, organizational arrangements, professional interrelationships, the development and present status of the profession and its obligations, and so on—must also be mastered.

Liberal Education

In recent decades the first of these essential components of the knowledge base of the profession, the concept of liberal education, has remained alive as a goal, but as a practice it has suffered much. Despite the failings of society and higher education that have contributed to the decline of commitment and performance in liberal education, the intellectual and moral dimensions of teaching as a profession make possession of a liberal education a *requirement* for a competent teacher.

The challenge of defining the goals of a liberal education arises primarily because of the diverse nature of the principal elements requiring inclusion. For example, one element refers to academic and scholarly content—that which is known and worth transmitting. Another refers to a fluid set of skills. Still another dimension treats values and attitudes that constitute the mark of educated persons and stand as the highest aspirations of humankind. A fourth element treats the ways in which teaching and learning are accomplished so that the recipient of a liberal education comes to understand the critical interconnections among content, skills, and purpose. The difficulty of defining the goals of a liberal education, therefore, lies in their dynamic character. A simple taxonomy is insufficient because of its discreteness. A listing belies the interconnections. The linear character of prose tends to conceal the interactive effects of the component parts.

In conceptual terms, the purpose of a liberal education may be divided into three broad areas. The first area is *literacy*, very broadly defined. By literacy I refer to an awareness of the several domains of knowledge and the modes of inquiry in terms of which further advances in knowledge are made. Those several domains include the natural and social sciences and the humanities. By literacy I also mean conversance with the structures and institutions—nationally and globally—of society, government, the economy, and technology. Literacy includes also the development of an understanding of the meaning of perspective as manifest, for example, in different eras, cultures, and roles. Finally, what might be called the concept of connectedness—the interrelationships among, for example, disciplines, cultures, times, and perspectives—is an important element in this broad goal of literacy.

A second broad area embraces *essential skills* that ought to be the aim of general education. While there are important skills implicit and, indeed, embedded in literacy (for example, the modes of inquiry by which knowledge is advanced), in this goal I mean to refer explicitly to the skills of thinking, analysis, synthesis, and communication. The goal is clear thinking, unambiguous presentation of thought and ideas, awareness of and facility with different modes of thinking—quantitative and qualitative—and the capacity to develop and critique arguments and to inquire and test the products of that inquiry. This goal includes attention to the development of skills for self-aware and independent learning, an absolutely essential instrument for all later learning. It includes attention to the concept of design as manifest in art, technology, and human affairs.

The third major goal addresses *values, purposes,* and *the requisites of action.* Just as ideas are stimuli to action, so too are values and a sense of the aesthetic. The purpose of preparation is to be found in the unavoidability of future action. Certainly one important way to view the context for education is in terms of crucial and continuing choices facing individuals and society. For some time now the world has lived in an era characterized by diverse attempts to initiate change. Yet complex interactions mean that even deliberate actions yield unpredictable impacts. Furthermore, the strings of action and reaction extend over long periods of time. In such an environment of change and unpredictability stand many choices, competing values, uncertain and pluralistic futures, and individuals, groups, and agencies as actors. One broad goal, therefore, of a general education ought to be attention to discourse on values, to individual self-knowledge as to purpose and priority, and to a conception of self as responsible actor and initiator, with capacities but also limits.

The goals stated here cannot be understood as standing by themselves. They cannot be understood as calling simply for courses in this or that subject and for so many credit hours. They must be understood as content in simultaneous relation to skills, purpose, and instructional approach—not just *what* is taught, but *how*, and with service to broader purposes clearly in mind.

Subject Matter Mastery

Not a great deal needs to be said, really, to further explicate content mastery as an essential component in the knowledge base of a teacher. It is impossible either to teach or to evaluate whether teaching has been successful without mastery of the subject.

Disciplinary Underpinnings of the Profession

There are, of course, many different ways of acquiring a liberal education. For educators, however, special focus needs to be given to the behavioral and social sciences and the humanities. As noted above, those entering teaching should possess a thorough exposure to the domains of inquiry that inform them about the nature of society, culture, and humanity. These disciplines explore the nature of human development and learning. They help establish the cultural contexts within which educational goals and objectives are defined and served. They afford the teacher essential understanding about children, not only in terms of their generic characteristics as learners, but also the cultural and familial diversity inevitably present in any given schooling situation that children encounter. The humanities complement the essentially reductionist character of much behavioral and social science and provide strategies for integrating what would otherwise be discrete information with the substance of our humanity, as we live and experience it.

Knowledge Associated with Professional Role

A liberal education, mastered content, and broad background in the behavioral and social sciences and the humanities are necessary but not sufficient. There is also a large and growing body of professional knowledge that must be mastered. The most direct way of defining this knowledge is in terms of the dimensions of professional role. The professional domains that we in teacher education should demonstrably master require a thorough knowledge of the following:

1. Different instructional approaches, including use of existing and emerging media.

2. The relationship between diverse characteristics of learners and instructional strategies.

3. Curriculum models and theories, especially as applied to all the subjects of instruction for which a given teacher will be responsible (for example, reading, wherever and however appropriate, as well as English, mathematics, science, art, or other areas).

4. Small-group processes.

5. Professional responsibilities and obligations.

6. Consultation skills to work with other professionals, including knowledge of their roles and the organization and administration of schools.

7. Parent/professional relations (including community relations).

8. A capacity for inquiry and design oriented toward the specific circumstances of individual learners at given times, including diagnosis, instructional and curricular design, and evaluation skills suited to the requirements of diagnosis and the validation of learning.

9. Classroom and behavior management (or whatever terms are more politically acceptable).

10. Self-awareness, or the capacities of intrapersonal skills, the ability
    to be in touch with oneself.

Reader and listener reactions to earlier versions of this chapter,
whether out of ignorance or sometimes outright rejection (for example, that there is [as one critic put it] "no foundation of esoteric
knowledge for pedagogy, such as exists for law and medicine"), make
it imperative that I at least "telegraph" the sources of the professional
knowledge base claimed above by mentioning the names of such
scholars as B. O. Smith, N. L. Gage, Thomas Good, Donald Medley,
Robert Soar, David Berliner, Jane Stallings, and Barak Rosenshine,
to name just a small but distinguished handful.

THE SETTINGS FOR TEACHING

Contradictions in Our Profession

Having defined the first essential premise, let me now turn to the
second. Examination of the settings to which our graduates go reveal
to us the serious contradictions inherent in our profession. The work
of Dan Lortie, supplemented by the insights of Robert Schaefer, is
instructive here.

Lortie's research on teachers, for example, has documented in great
and fascinating detail how, of three kinds of rewards—extrinsic (for
example, salary), ancillary (for example, holiday schedules and sum-
mers free), and psychic and intrinsic (for example, satisfaction in
helping children learn)—far and away the most overwhelmingly
important to teachers is the last.[1] The profession itself, however, is
characterized by easy entry and what Lortie calls an unstepped
nature of the career line. We all know what the first means—
unfortunately. What the second means is that aside from salary steps
or advancement out of teaching into specialized roles or administration, there is very little differentiation within the teaching roles and far
fewer displays of deference than found in other professions in the
presence of greater experience or high-quality performance. To these
characteristics, unfortunate as they are by themselves, can be added a
third drawn from Schaefer's work.[2] He notes the contradiction between, on the one hand, the nature of the task (intellectual) and the
academic character of the education required to prepare for the task,

and, on the other, the isolated, nonscholarly, and non-self-renewing character of the setting in which teaching takes place. While there are, to be sure, intrinsic rewards in teaching, as a professional activity it is not designed, in its structure and process, to be continuously self-renewing and professionally developmental. Rarely does a teacher's personal experience contribute to the larger profession; in very few settings is it affected by peer influences or the collegial processes common to other professions.

An Unavoidable Conclusion

I have briefly sketched what we know and what teachers must know as they enter the profession. *But what do we do?* We take seventeen- and eighteen-year-olds and try, *in just four short years*, to equip the best-qualified candidates we can attract with a liberal education of breadth and substance, with a firm underpinning in the academic disciplines essential to the science and art of teaching, and with an understanding of the complexity and diversity of human learning and development. Moreover, we strive to instill in these teacher candidates a sense of the social and cultural contexts of schooling, to foster professional skills in curriculum, instruction, and classroom management, and to provide them with at least one full quarter of intensive, full-time practicum in student teaching.

The conclusion is unavoidable. *Teacher education as it is currently practiced in the United States—a four-year baccalaureate enterprise—is attempting to accomplish the impossible.*

That is why I began by arguing that we require a revolution in our profession. Nothing less will suffice. Think for a moment, though, of the word *revolution*. In colloquial use it means a radical change, without antecedents, constituting a sharp break with the past. But all revolutions have occurred within a specific cultural and historical context, and all have been constrained by their pasts—by the conditions that engendered them. So it must be with the image of the revolution in teaching and teacher education outlined here.

The Current Situation

We are expected to accomplish the goals of teacher education with resources not adequate to the task. These resources are of four kinds: student talent, student time, money, and academic and professional faculty.

The decline in the entry qualifications of teaching candidates is well documented. It is serious, though not as damaging to the profession as some would have us believe. I know of no programs, for example, that have lowered their entry standards in recent years. I know of many where entering students are closer to the minimum qualifications long specified. This distinction is important. Our situation is unfortunate, but it is not unethical or irresponsible.

The amount of student time available to teacher educators is the second inadequacy. In no way can the levels of proficiency we must come to demand be achieved in four years. We must do more than merely expose teacher candidates to the wide knowledge they need; we must require that they become masters of how to use that knowledge.

The bleak financial history of teacher education has also been well documented. Teacher education programs, long the financial beasts of burden for their institutions, were expected to provide students and generate resources that could then support other programs. The consequences of the heavy instructional load that teacher education faculties were expected to carry—never mind that we should have been following clinical models—drew us away from critical inquiry and scholarship and slowed the development of the knowledge bases for teaching.

Equally important as the three areas of inadequacy outlined above is the degree to which institutions and public education authorities have been willing to sanction teacher education programs with faculty resources spread too thinly to educate teachers properly. The intellectual underpinnings of teaching are far broader than can be represented by a mere handful of faculty members. Perhaps some form of guided apprenticeship training might be possible, but an intellectually sound professional education is out of the question.[3]

I can almost hear the outrage. How can I dismiss small teacher education programs so easily? Who says they are less adequate than the larger ones? Where is the evidence?

In fact, I cannot say that larger or smaller programs are better or worse because neither type is achieving the kind of preparation I have in mind. But if the foundations of teacher education are as broad and as deep as I maintain they are, how can as few as five faculty members provide an adequate program? Are there any faculties of law, medicine, or engineering numbering as few as five members? And five is not a magic number; I suspect that the minimum number in other professional faculties is much larger.

In any case, the proposal I want to sketch cannot entail the closing of any teacher education programs in the near future—certainly not until the new models have been designed, tested, and installed. The revolution I am calling for will take decades to accomplish, and virtually every institution now educating teachers will continue to educate at least as many students as it does now.

A REVOLUTIONARY PROPOSAL

The more I reflect on the problems and opportunities now facing us, the more I am convinced that the entry-level professional training of teachers should take a minimum of six years beyond high school. Moreover, I believe that the breadth of knowledge and the level of societal demands on the teaching profession require, in most schools, a hierarchical arrangement of teaching roles. A new role of *lead teacher* must be defined, and the occupants of these new positions must be expected to undergo further professional training equivalent to two additional years before they assume their responsibilities. The first major element of the revolution, therefore, consists of placing entry into professional training at the *end* of the undergraduate sequence rather than at the beginning. The second entails *restructuring of the workplace* of the teacher in order that, in the delivery of instruction as well as in the performance of other professional functions, the currently available knowledge base can be operationalized.

Extending Professional Education

Let me consider these two elements in more detail. A strong case can be made that the liberal education goals, including mastery in content areas, call for more than enough course work to fill the four-year undergraduate experience. There is simply not enough time to achieve professional goals during these same four years. However, the undergraduate experience of those who anticipate becoming teacher candidates ought to include some exposure to the teaching profession. There should be limited course offerings, therefore, at the junior or senior level that give students firsthand experience in the schools. In addition, as part of the liberal education curriculum, students should study policy and organizational and societal issues arising out of and directly related to schooling. Such courses should be broadly focused so that students not intending to teach might also enroll.

A significant advantage of this proposal is that it draws a clearer line between, on the one hand, the liberal education/content area responsibilities of teacher preparation and, on the other, the professional component of training. At least part of the problem with the education of teachers has been the erosion of the responsibility of arts and sciences faculties for maintaining the definition, design, and curricular standards of a liberal education. As my stance on liberal education goals clearly implies, merely providing opportunities for meeting distribution requirements is not enough. By making entry to professional preparation conditional upon a completed liberal education, teacher educators can influence the program offered by arts and sciences.

The basic professional education sequence that would follow the baccalaureate degree would take a minimum of two full academic years. It would include, at a deeper level than is now possible, didactic and clinical instruction in the entire range of professional skills listed earlier. Let me incorporate, by specific reference at this point, the profoundly stimulating proposals of B. O. Smith's *A Design for a School of Pedagogy*. They are far and away the most comprehensive and valuable set of suggestions bearing on professional preparation in our necessary revolution. The period of professional training would conclude with an intensive internship in a special school designed and operated cooperatively by the teacher training institution and local education agencies. Such a setting would provide a great deal more observation and supportive clinical analysis of teaching than is available to teacher candidates today.[4]

I base my argument for the two-year postbaccalaureate training program on the extent of the existing knowledge base—that which is known and of value to the professional repertoire of a well-prepared teacher. Suppose for the sake of argument that for each of the separate professional skill areas, we offered a minimum of one solid course.[5] That would mean, for example, one course in curriculum models and theories, one course in instructional approaches and media, one course in small-group processes, and so forth. The number of such courses, conservatively estimated, might be ten. Suppose we also insist on a solid foundation in the academic disciplines because they underpin the science and art of teaching—history, philosophy and ethics, psychology, sociology, political science, biology and neurology, anthropology, economics, and the arts. We arrive very quickly at five full quarters of academic work. Allow one quarter for a teaching internship (perhaps one quarter is not enough), and my proposal seems spare indeed.

But even this proposal suffices only to prepare *entering* professionals; it says nothing about transforming workplace settings so that they become sufficiently stimulating intellectually to foster the retention of trained teachers or to assure their continuing professional development. There is little point in developing a new and more expensive model for initial training in a profession as complex as teaching without also considering the means of providing for the retention of such teachers or for ongoing development as part and parcel of a teacher's professional life. These two aims of retention and continued development can occur only if we seriously address the redefinition of the structure of schools.

Restructuring the School Environment

Consider, therefore, the setting in which teaching takes place—the school environment. How must schools be organized so that persons trained to higher levels of professional sophistication will be willing to stay in them? How can we make our new breed of teachers feel that their skills are being effectively employed? The answer is deceptively simple: *The school must be transformed into a setting for professional employment.* We must be hardheaded here, however. Though we might wish it to be otherwise, teaching is now only a semiprofession. Accepting this judgment is difficult, given the level of educational preparation required to enter teaching. But the facts remain. We cannot demonstrate that throughout our ranks we act on a base of warrantable knowledge. We cannot display the kinds of day-to-day professional interactions that characterize other professions. We cannot demonstrate that an abiding theme guiding our daily functions is a collective orientation to improvement of performance. We cannot show that we are weeding out of the profession on an ongoing basis those who do not perform at the state of the art or who display unwillingness to maintain their skills at such a level. Until our day-to-day functioning is characterized in such a fashion, we will neither be entitled to nor achieve professional status.

To accomplish these objectives, schools must come to be composed of hierarchically structured teams of teachers. Those trained for initial entry in the new program would be supervised by practicing lead teachers responsible for up to 200 children and for as many as seven to ten professionals. (Such a structure, it is important to note, would allow overall student/teacher ratios to be much the same as they are now.)

Each large unit would be solely responsible for the children in its charge—save that certain specialized curricular expertise would be needed from time to time. Problems unresolved at the level of the staff teachers—whether curricular, instructional, parental, or behavioral—would be resolved by the lead teacher. Each unit would be responsible for planning, carrying out, and evaluating the instruction it offers and for monitoring the progress of individual children. Lead teachers would be responsible for the following:

1. Facilitating the planning and evaluation activities of the teaching unit.

2. Organizing instruction.

3. Applying appropriate inquiry strategies to individual diagnosis and instructional design.

4. Keeping up with instructional research and development and transmitting its fruits to the teaching staff as an integral part of planning, design, and evaluation activities.

5. Maintaining relations with parents.

6. Troubleshooting.

7. Maintaining relations with district specialists and the building administrator.

8. Developing schoolwide plans and budget proposals, in association with other lead teachers, representative parents, and administrators.

9. Evaluating and supervising staff teachers.

Such a hierarchical teaching arrangement would provide a new way of offering differential salaries and might help prevent teachers from leaving teaching altogether in order to advance themselves. In addition, it would end the isolation of individual teachers and provide a means for staff development within the teaching setting. Moreover, though there would be an investment, the costs should be manageable.

Some might—and have—criticized this proposal as merely adding to the bureaucratization of schooling or as differentiated staffing revisited. Others may claim that the present responsibilities of teachers include most of the functions called for in the lead teacher role.

In part that is true, of course, but it is a truth that corresponds to advances achieved by other professions, for example, medicine, which launched its advance in the nineteenth century in part by successfully distinguishing the roles of pharmacist, nurse, and surgeon from that of the physician. Furthermore, those who may classify the proposed lead teacher roles as roles that properly belong to the principal or a department chairperson blithely ignore the reality of current school organizational impediments that effectively prevent those functions from being performed. Until such time when the splendid isolation of teachers is effectively ended, through organizational models and the arrangement of physical space that corresponds to the requirements and opportunities of those organizational models, little beyond marginal improvements is likely to occur. Effective action based on what is known will not be possible, nor will sufficient incentives to attract more capable and better qualified practitioners come to exist.

What kinds of persons could perform the lead roles identified above? Certainly not inexperienced teachers or persons who had only those formal skills and knowledge transmitted in a two-year training program. The full extent of the professional knowledge base available to ground and support the teaching role is far greater than can be acquired in two years. Excellence and expertise in *all* the domains of professional skill, which ought to be directly available to every child through the structured team approach I have outlined, cannot be developed in any individual in less than four years of intensive study and clinical practice. For the higher-level and broader skills called for in the lead teacher role, at least two years of formal training after several years of successful practice would be required. Lead teachers must be trained at a level equivalent to a professional doctorate, they should be paid accordingly, and when they are, we will finally have the needed incentives to keep the most successful and capable practitioners in a teaching career.[6]

The Litany of Objections

Obstacles in the path of the proposal are numerous. We have all heard the litany of objections before. Let me rehearse each, along with a responsive reading.

1. *We will not recruit better students, especially for postbaccalaureate programs, until the financial rewards of teaching are higher.*

By and large, students choose teaching for reasons other than salary. Witness the continuing availability of teachers in the private teaching sector, which pays notoriously less than the public. Money is far less important than the quality of the environment and the intrinsic rewards, such as the opportunities for continued professional growth and for peer interaction. Even so, the proposed parallel restructuring of the teaching setting would create the opportunity for career development *within* teaching with appropriate accompanying financial reward.

2. *The knowledge base of teacher education is nonexistent.*

The knowledge base for teaching *does* exist. To assert otherwise may be only to argue the uselessness of much that passes for educational research, or to cover for one's own failure to keep abreast of developments, or to believe that an apprenticeship model is more appropriate, or to reveal one's own lack of awareness, or some combination of these. Still, the behavioral and social sciences and the arts have a great deal to contribute to the training of teachers, and real advances have been made in the curricular, evaluation, and instructional practices of education. This is not to say that there is not room for a great deal more—and more sophisticated—thinking about what it means to have a knowledge base for teaching and, given that meaning, what one should then do. It is striking that other professions do not appear to worry as much as we do about their epistemological underpinnings; perhaps that is a symbol of their relative maturity.

However, I do not believe that is the whole story. What we in our human and social service profession are up to is in many ways far more complicated than—to say nothing of being qualitatively different from—what lawyers, engineers, and physicians are called upon to do. Lawyers, for example, operate within the boundaries of a designed system called the law, and while there is plenty of room for the exercise of creativity and imagination, the framework remains a designed system of law, jurisprudence, and the concept of precedent. Physicians and engineers each operate, on the whole, in terms of knowledge that is far more tractable in its discovery and in its application than anything we might wish to rely on in our domain. Educators deal with variables far more holistic in character; moreover, we face the difficulty of having to form partnerships with the objects of our attention, which is quite unlike anything an engineer may be required to do with structural steel or the physician with the physiological processes he or she is seeking to regulate and normalize in a patient.

It is also pertinent to note that not only is the knowledge different, but we have not, for a variety of reasons, given as much attention as is needed to what it means to "stand on the knowledge base." Clearly, that phrase is a metaphor and a multifaceted one at that. Theoretical knowledge, for example, requires translation into practical terms: this is something teachers are no more likely to be capable of doing than is the average engineer in translating the principles of physics and chemistry directly into the design of bridges or skyscrapers. Knowledge may require, as has been argued here, transformation of the organization of the school, something clearly beyond the scope of individual teacher action. Knowledge may entail the transformation, not of practice but of attitude, a difficult and sensitive task at best. These comments are meant only to be illustrative. There is a vast terrain to consider here, and it has been traversed only lightly. The central message, however, is not that we cannot do it, but that to argue that there is no demonstrated knowledge base to guide us borders on professional irresponsibility.

3. *Teachers are born, not made.*
Yes, teachers are born. Most are made. The task is to provide the requisite tools to the 98 percent of teachers who must work at being successful.

4. *Political factors will stall and eventually kill this proposal; in the end, narrow self-interest will prevail.*
As for politics, I love 'em. But I am sick of the use of the political argument as a wet blanket for dousing the spark of potentially powerful ideas. We in education must assert the primacy of knowledge and intellect over mere expediency.

5. *Who, trained to the levels you propose, would work in schools as they now exist?*
Retaining in our present school structure candidates trained to the level I am proposing would indeed be a problem. The solution lies in the changed structure of the schools I have proposed.

6. *Small programs will be put out of business.*

Certainly, we cannot put small programs out of business. In the long run, however, maintaining small teacher education programs will not be professionally possible. Fortunately, the proposed model will allow smaller institutions now engaging in teacher education to concentrate on the baccalaureate-level liberal education and content mastery. Indeed, smaller schools may well prove to be far better equipped than larger institutions to provide this kind of instruction. Liberal education conceived as I have presented it here requires continuous negotiation, deliberation, and monitoring, within and across academic disciplines. Such activities seem to be very difficult, if not impossible, to sustain in the larger, multipurpose institutions with their competing aims and purposes.

PERSPECTIVES ON CHANGE

At this stage, my proposal may appear overly formidable. From the perspective, however, of the thirty or forty years it will require to refine and put the model into practice, it appears incremental. First, we must formulate specific designs. Then, a handful of universities must arrange with local school systems to create the new school organizations as demonstration and training sites. The success of these sites will generate a demand for additional ones. Gradually, changes will occur in professional certification, local and state regulations, and national accreditation. No magic wand will bring these proposals to life. Over time, what seems revolutionary in conception will appear incremental and deliberate in implementation.

Can we really accomplish all of this? Let me cite an outstanding parallel, offered not as an argument that we should follow its processes as a model, but for the historical insight it affords.

Consider the following description by an internationally known figure in higher education of the way in which degree candidates were examined and admitted to a certain profession in 1876.

In these professional colleges generally, a very light examination is imposed upon the students. I have seen at a professional faculty, composed of gentlemen of good reputation, the following process. There were nine departments in which examinations were conducted, every one important to the purpose. The nine examiners sat around a table. Each examiner had a piece of cardboard, on one side of which was a big black round spot; the other side was white. The rule was that the candidate who had passed in the majority of nine subjects should be admitted to his degree; and in order to prevent negative votes, as they were given, from influencing the minds of the examiners who had not voted, all the gentlemen voted simultaneously. The dean of the faculty gave the name: "John Jones. Are you ready to vote? Vote." Each man slapped out his card. If black, it was against the candidate, if white, for him. If five black spots appeared the candidate was rejected; if only four, he received his degree. The successful candidate might have been entirely ignorant of four out of the nine subjects.[7]

Consider the following testimony about this same profession:

It is . . . humiliating to make a comparison of economic and social position of our leading members . . . with leading lawyers and other professional men.[8]

or

The income of many a member (of the same profession) who has spent years in acquiring a professional education is often less than an ordinary mechanic.[9]

Things were not much better for this profession six years later. Consider the entrance requirements for it at the following universities, as reported in 1910 by Flexner in his study of medical education:[10]

Columbia University—a high school diploma (p. 268)
New York University—a high school diploma (p. 269)
University of Michigan—two years of college (p. 243)
University of Pittsburgh—a high school diploma (p. 297)
Harvard University—a baccalaureate degree (p. 240)
Boston University—a high school diploma or examination "markedly below the four year high school standard" (p. 241)
Temple University—less than a high school diploma (p. 295).

I have been describing the profession of medicine. The university president of world renown was Charles W. Eliot. I quoted him from Abraham Flexner's biography of Daniel Coit Gilman, who is widely regarded as responsible for creating the model for medical education at Johns Hopkins University, a model that Flexner used as the template for his study of medical education, which irrevocably transformed the preparation of physicians and surgeons in North America.

Before the beginning of the nineteenth century, there were only five medical schools in America. Training proceeded according to an apprenticeship model; success, therefore, depended on the master. A library was important and so was a hospital. The system of medical training gradually evolved into a proprietary one, with local medical societies or groups of doctors organizing a typically two-year course as a business venture. While we now think of medical education as a four-year course, medical historian Saul Benison wryly notes that the first four-year medical course in America was the War between the States.[11]

The first steps at reform were taken by Eliot at Harvard when he moved to take the very successful proprietary medical college under the wing of the university. He sought a graded medical curriculum at Harvard, finally getting what he wanted after a two-year struggle. It would be twenty years, however, before Harvard expanded its two-year program to a three-year one. It was *twenty-five* years before students stopped observing experiments in clinical amphitheaters and began performing them themselves. Finally, in the 1890s Harvard succeeded in having all its students present baccalaureate degrees at entry, but even under President Abbott Laurence Lowell, who succeeded Eliot in 1909, there were still arguments that two years of college work would be enough.

At Johns Hopkins University the pattern was somewhat different. There the key was the hospital and the man who founded it, John Shaw Billings. Billings was one of the physicians who received his most important training at "Civil War Medical College." After the war he joined the Surgeon General's Office and undertook the task of upgrading military hospitals. He also upgraded the library of the Surgeon General's office, transforming it into a master catalogue and a device for transmitting knowledge in the fashion of an index medica. This was a major step toward standardizing medical knowledge and the creation of handbooks that characterize developed professions.

Gilman hired Billings in the 1870s to plan the Johns Hopkins Hospital, the necessary adjunct to the medical school that Gilman planned for his university. The hospital opened and operated well before the opening of a medical school, which was distinguished in that it would require a bachelor's degree of all its students and would also admit women. All the degree candidates would be schooled in the sciences by faculty members, many of whom had been trained at the great European universities. A key distinguishing feature of these two departures was that the medical faculty were not only engaged in the transmission of clinical knowledge and skill, but were also deeply engaged in the production of medical knowledge at the same time. Thus it was that over a hundred years ago Charles Eliot of Harvard University and Daniel Coit Gilman of Johns Hopkins University set about the reform of medical education in the United States. Their reasoning was exactly analogous to mine with respect to teacher education. They decided to create programs of medical education founded on the extant and developing knowledge of the biological sciences, committed to inquiry in the conduct of medical education, and connected to a hospital under the control of the teaching faculty. Instead of accepting students with a high school diploma, they insisted on a baccalaureate degree. Instead of a two-year program, they insisted on four.

Thirty-four years later, when Abraham Flexner undertook a rating of the medical schools in North America, he used Johns Hopkins as the model. Even so, it was another twenty years before the baccalaureate entry requirement and the four-year program became universal. That was a mere two generations ago.

If we in teacher education begin today, what can we not accomplish by the turn of the century?

NOTES

1. See Dan Lortie, *Schoolteacher: A Sociological Study* (Chicago: University of Chicago Press, 1975).
2. See Robert J. Schaefer, *The School as a Center of Inquiry* (New York: Harper & Row, 1967).
3. Let me make a brief aside. One of the perennial puzzles respecting those who argue that apprenticeship is the proper approach to teacher training is their failure to follow through on the implications of their claim. If one examines closely what apprenticeship means in the trades, one finds the expenditure of periods of time extending over years, a process designed to acquaint the apprentices with the full range of challenges and skills they are likely to encounter, and close supervision on virtually a one-to-one basis. Given the liberal education and content mastery requirements for educating teachers, a true apprenticeship model would have to begin after the baccalaureate experience and then extend for years after that! Few proponents of the apprenticeship approach show awareness of the substantial implicit costs.
4. See B. O. Smith, *A Design for a School of Pedagogy* (Washington, D.C.: U.S. Government Printing Office, 1980).
5. I recognize the danger that in referring to a "course" I may be presumed to be

pressing for old models of didactic instruction at the expense of clinical and
field-based experiences as well. As those who have read Smith know, I do not
mean to suggest anything of the sort. The realities of the organization, financial
support, and allocation of instructional load in higher education will recognize
that reference to "courses" is a necessary, administrative shorthand evil.

6. This proposal may be compared with Lawrence A. Cremin's in his "The
   Education of the Educating Profession," in *The Knowledge Base for the Preparation
   of Education Personnel, vol. 1* (Washington, D.C.: American Association of Colleges
   of Teacher Education, 1978), pp. 5–24; and the more recent formulation by
   Donna H. Kerr in her "Teaching Competence and Teacher Education in the
   United States," *Teachers College Record* 84 (Spring 1983): 525–52.

7. Abraham Flexner, *Daniel Coit Gilman* (New York: Harcourt, Brace, 1946),
   pp. 112–13.

8. From *Pittsburgh Medical Review* (June 1876), as quoted in Robert B. Howsam et
   al., *Entering a Profession* (Washington, D.C.: American Association of Colleges for
   Teacher Education, 1976), p. 33.

9. From *Cosmopolitan* (April 1903) as quoted in Howsam et al., *Entering a Profession*,
   p. 33.

10. See Abraham Flexner, *Medical Education in the United States and Canada* (Washing-
    ton, D.C.: Carnegie Foundation for the Advancement of Teaching, 1910).

11. Saul Benison, personal communication, 1981.

3

Teacher Education: A Perspective from a Major Public University

John R. Palmer

INTRODUCTION

In the last half of the nineteenth century, public universities became an increasingly significant part of higher education in the United States. The individual states responded to the stimulus provided by the federal initiative embodied in the concept of a land-grant institution, a university designed to serve the needs of a developing society. What were perceived as the practical arts—areas of study such as engineering, agriculture, and teacher training—were emphasized in the enabling legislation in the states and tended to distinguish these new universities from the existing private institutions that were rooted in classical curricula.

Despite the perceived need on the part of state legislators and the public for better teachers, the development of departments of teacher education within the new public universities was a slow and often difficult process. Individual professors interested in pedagogy offered courses or lectures sporadically, and often not as part of a systematic program of teacher training. Training programs that were established tended to disappear after a few years. Then, as now, public universities were not certain how to deal with teacher education or if they even wanted it. Only the public demand for a supply of well-educated teachers prevented many public universities from relegating teacher education entirely to less prestigious state colleges and normal schools. The low status of teacher training in state universities was established early, and it has persisted. It continues to be a primary factor in determining the resources, the faculty, and the student body available to schools and colleges of education. It is a paradox that universities in this country have often treated with disdain the preparation of individuals to assist the young in their intellectual development. One might expect universities to view teacher preparation as one of their most significant tasks, one to be given the highest priority, but such has not been the case.

While progress in the development of departments of pedagogy was very uneven in the early years of public universities, by the 1920s the pattern of separate units devoted primarily to the preparation of personnel for the public schools was clearly established. Departments of education or programs of teacher preparation were often initially located in arts and science colleges, but they rapidly took on an independent status. While remnants of the earlier ties to the arts and science faculty and college still remain, by the 1950s colleges of education had become major independent units in most public universities. Indeed, the sharp increase in the birth rate following World War II created such a need for teachers that as many as one-fourth of college students enrolled in public universities were teacher education majors. Teacher education had become the largest task of higher education, and schools of education often became the second largest unit in the university, exceeded in size of faculty and student body only by the arts and science college. Whether they wished to or not, university administrators had to reckon with such a large part of their enterprise.

The last decade has seen a very different trend in enrollment patterns, and professional education units have typically lost whatever advantage they had because of their size relative to other units within the university. Students, particularly academically able women, have shifted from teacher preparation programs and related courses in the arts and science college to majors in agriculture, business,

engineering, and the health professions. In the 1950s national surveys of college freshmen revealed that 20 to 30 percent of them hoped
to become elementary or secondary school teachers. Those figures
have now dropped to 2 to 4 percent. There are many reasons for
this dramatic shift, some of which are quite beyond the control of
schools of education, but the impact on those schools is profound.
Only a few years ago, sheer numbers protected schools of education
despite their low status in the world of higher education, but that protection is now gone, and they have become vulnerable to attack from
within the university as well as from outside.

Perhaps the important point to make relative to this most recent
shift in the fortunes of schools of education is that long-term predictions about professional education units in universities should be
viewed very cautiously. Such units do appear to be tied rather closely
to some historically persistent realities—the low status of teachers in
the United States; the supply-demand situation, which is directly
related to the birth rate; and the status of pedagogy as a field of
research in universities; assumptions about funding professional preparation of teachers, as compared with the preparation of lawyers or
physicians. But there are other factors that can and do change quickly
that affect the total circumstances of a school of education in a public
university. To state the point another way, the circumstances described in this overview may come to change so substantially in a
decade that the observations made here will be of little value in, say,
the year 1990. In a period of very rapid social and economic change,
this same observation can probably be made about many social
institutions.

Whether any speculations about the future hold true, it is the case
that schools of education in public research universities are con-
fronted today with a number of circumstances and problems that
must be addressed. The remainder of this chapter is devoted to an
analysis of some of those circumstances and problems.

THE MISSION

While it may seem odd, schools of education now face a problem in
defining their mission. What are the limits of professional education?
Typically, we have been concerned with what goes on in schools, and

particularly with preparing the personnel who work in schools. But the schools comprise only a part of education. Business, industry, and health care organizations now have huge educational enterprises that, in size, in some cases match those of most states or large cities. Educators may be found in almost any large organization, and it appears that the retraining of millions of workers in the United States in the decades ahead will enlarge the number of educators working outside traditional school systems.

Should education faculty be training individuals for nonschool as well as school settings? For many years, of course, persons trained to work in schools have at the outset or even midway through their careers taken positions in settings other than school systems, readily transferring their acquired knowledge and skills to the demands of nonschool educational roles. But should schools of education deliberately train students for such roles? Should another array of courses and curricula be developed specifically for such training?

It is not at all clear that education faculty have yet mastered the task of preparing individuals to staff elementary and secondary schools, the traditional and central responsibility assigned such faculties when schools of education were founded earlier in this century. The task remains an important and difficult one. School teachers, administrators, counselors, and other professional staff make up one of the largest groups of professionals in this country. Developing collegiate programs that assure state taxpayers who support such programs that their schools are staffed with competent, effective individuals has proved to be a demanding task. In recent years many critics have said schools of education are failing in this task. If this is true, is it not enough to work at this task and regain the confidence of the public in this most obvious area of responsibility?

Still, some argue that the need for training personnel for nonschool roles is there, and further ask, who is better equipped to train educators than an education faculty? A number of studies have demonstrated that the skills and knowledge needed to develop and operate educational programs in business, industry, and health care agencies are virtually carbon copies of those needed in the schools. Needs assessment, course development, teaching skills, assessment of learning outcomes, evaluation of teaching performance—these and other activities occur in almost all nonschool as well as school settings. To be sure, the students are usually adults rather than children, but adult education has been an accepted part of professional education for many years. The principles of human learning and effective teaching are similar regardless of the age or experience of the student, although significant adjustments must be made from group to group.

As other chapters in this volume deal in detail with the role of schools of education in the preparation of personnel for human service settings, the matter will not be addressed further here. Every major public university will have to deal with the issue, however. The need for educational personnel in nonschool settings is large and growing. Public institutions will be forced to respond, to serve the public need, and a key decision will be whether to reshape schools of education to assume new responsibilities or create a new unit or units elsewhere in the university. In some states the decision has already been made, while in others things are happening simply by chance, without planning or a recognition of the need. In such situations it is very likely that within a decade the school of education will find on the campus another faculty that largely duplicates the areas of expertise of the existing school of education faculty.

WHAT IS A PROFESSIONAL SCHOOL?

The writings of Clark Kerr, president of the University of California at Berkeley in the 1960s, brought into focus the unique characteristics of the very large public multiversities that have developed in the United States. Rather than being tightly knit, homogeneous institutions, multiversities can better be described as a group of loosely affiliated independent colleges and schools that occupy adjacent buildings, yet exist within a shared administrative and budgetary structure. The differences among them are as significant as what they hold in common. One set of fundamental differences is that which exists between professional schools and the units representing the basic natural and social sciences, humanities, and the arts.

Professional school faculty and programs have purposes that differ from those of many other units in the university. While they may prepare research scholars, their primary mission has been to prepare practitioners, that is, individuals who upon leaving the university will be lawyers, business people, physicians, or elementary and secondary school teachers. Programs offered by, say, the physics department, on the other hand, are designed primarily to prepare research scholars who will work in other universities or in the private sector. As a consequence, the professional concerns of the faculty of a professional school are typically quite different from those of physics professors. Law professors, for example, are very concerned about reading and producing research, but they also must be concerned about the practice of law, about the state bar, and about whatever changes are occurring in the society that influence the law and lawyers. A physics professor qua physics professor has much more limited concerns.

In addition to reading and producing research, faculty in schools of education are expected to devote much time and attention to the teaching profession and its needs, to whatever is occurring within schools and the society generally that has import for the preparation of school personnel. Such activity tends to draw the attention of education faculty away from basic research and other traditional scholarly activities and toward the problem of practitioners and schools. Practical questions replace theoretical questions as the research agenda of many faculty. Applied rather than basic research may dominate the research program. The time that is given to working with practitioners is time taken away from research and scholarly writing. Presentation of material focused on the practice of pedagogy creeps into course syllabi, replacing presentation of research or analysis of theoretical issues. Unfortunately, within the value system dominant in research universities, this is all viewed as undesirable.

Is its professional and practical orientation one that should be avoided by school of education faculty? It certainly should be if one desires to gain status within the university. But it certainly should not be if one wants to be respected and sought out by the teacher in the schools. Herein lies a major dilemma for many school of education faculty in public research universities. Am I to develop my career in order to be admired by other scholars in similar universities (and by faculty outside the school of education on my own campus) or to be admired by teachers and other school personnel who recognize the value of my efforts in their work and who appreciate my willingness to work with them and address their concerns? While there are many exceptions, faculty who choose to remain in research universities tend to respond to the value system of that institution, while the education faculty who spend their careers in state colleges and the smaller, private, liberal arts colleges tend to respond to the value system of the practitioner in the schools. But whatever decision the individual faculty member in the research university makes in this regard, he or she pays a price. Many faculty remain ambivalent throughout their careers. As a result of this ambivalence, they become less effective than they otherwise would be.

What is to be done about this situation? In his widely read monograph *A Design for a School of Pedagogy*, B. O. Smith makes a frontal assault on the problem and proposes a radical solution.[1] He suggests that fundamental errors were made when professional education was introduced into the universities of this country. These errors must be corrected now by radical surgery that will separate the preparation of teachers from the mainstream of the research university. The school of pedagogy should have its own criteria for faculty selection and promotion and should build its academic programs to meet the needs of school personnel rather than the needs of arts and science departments. In certain respects, Smith is calling for a return to the normal school concept. But perhaps a more appropriate analogy may be made by examining the place of schools of law and medicine in state university systems. Even though these schools exist within these systems, they function as very independent units with unique policies and procedures. Because of their status they have been able to maintain their independence from the arts and science faculty and its rules and procedures. They have responded to their own needs, not to the needs of the rest of the university.

While Smith's analysis of the difficulties education faculties have had surviving under the dominant value system of the research university is quite accurate, his proposed solution has many problems as well. It does, however, continue professional education as a university function, a very critical point. The formal education of every citizen is important to the life of an industrial society soon to be dominated by high technology, and it seems all but impossible to argue that education is not of primary import for such a society. It follows then that the training of teachers and other school personnel is of vital concern to this nation. Such training cannot be mediocre, and it must be conducted by the best that our system of higher education has to offer. This means future educators should take their collegiate work from the faculties in the major public and private universities, not in specialized institutions that are almost certain to employ faculty unable to get or hold positions in the more prestigious universities.

Whatever problems may have been created by the development of schools of education in major public universities, it has placed future teachers in the classes of many of the best scholars in the United States and, indeed, the world. It is important that that possibility remains. It is also important that students entering major research universities retain the option of becoming elementary or secondary school teachers. These universities attract a high-quality student body, some of whom during their undergraduate experience will decide to become teachers.

Professional schools will continue to be somewhat out of place in the major public research universities. Their mission will always be somewhat different from that of the other academic units of the university. But the gains associated with being part of the larger institution outweigh the problems. This is particularly true for the field of education, which carries a relatively low social status.

THE TRAINING OF TEACHERS

If the primary goals of a college education in the nineteenth century were to discipline and furnish the mind, the goal has now become one of preparing for a vocation. Regardless of what the faculty may wish or believe, students know that they are preparing for a vocation. They are preoccupied with the question, "What am I going to be?" Any course that does not appear to have direct application to a vocational goal becomes suspect and is likely to be eliminated from students' programs. It seems odd, indeed, to defend a course on the grounds that it will enhance the mental faculties of memory, imagination, or reasoning.

But as we have quite properly moved away from mental discipline in selecting the undergraduate curriculum, have we thrown out the baby of intellectual development with the bath of mental discipline? And as we have responded to the needs of a vocation, have we neglected the general education of prospective teachers? It may seem strange to question the vocational emphasis for prospective teachers. A collegiate program designed for teachers should prepare one for teaching, to be proficient in the art of teaching. Surely this is vocationalism at its best. But the question is, "What academic program best prepares a teacher for teaching?"

For several decades there was an apparent consensus on this question. A good deal of experimenting was done, to be sure, but as faculties of education grew and became independent units within universities, similar patterns for preparing educational personnel developed. The core of concern for the prospective teachers included human learning, human development, history or philosophy of education, teaching methods, some form of practice with children in an actual classroom, and a collection of courses taken from one or several academic disciplines to prepare the student to be proficient in the subject or subjects to be taught. In recent years, however, confidence in this pattern of courses has been badly shaken. No new consensus has developed, but a vigorous debate has begun, one that is rooted ultimately in the nature of teaching and the function of the teacher in and out of the classroom.

Every human being is a teacher, probably with some degree of success. Although we have all engaged in informal teaching of playmates, of our children, or of fellow workers, we also recognize that some have teaching as their primary occupation. As these individuals work at perfecting their teaching skills, they continue to utilize many of the techniques and strategies we all have used in our informal teaching. Teaching has always been a very common "natural" act, as essential to the life of primitive tribes as it is to our contemporary technological society.

But throughout this century, and particularly in the last decade or two, a group of researchers has begun to generate knowledge about teaching that goes well beyond the common sense of human experience. Teaching is becoming a technical field supported by a body of theory that must be learned and practiced before one can be certified as a teacher. This scientific body of knowledge requires careful study; and, as is the case with any science, at certain points it defies or appears contrary to common sense. Teacher preparation courses then must take on a new character, and the assessment of who is prepared to teach is determined by the knowledge of the principles of the science of teaching.

This challenge to the traditional approach to teacher preparation has occurred, by chance, at the same time the public has questioned the quality of the teachers currently in the schools. Is it possible the effectiveness of teachers would be greatly enhanced by emphasizing the science of teaching as defined by recent research studies? Some educators believe that it would.

There are others, however, who would look elsewhere for a solution to the public's questions. Teaching is not primarily a technical task dominated by specialized knowledge and behaviors unique to the teaching role. It is a uniquely human task requiring the exercise of intelligence, thought, and concern in the complex human interactions that vary infinitely among students and teachers. While the study of the teaching-learning context is useful, the study of literature, the arts, philosophy, and social and natural sciences may be more essential to the making of a teacher. Technique has little value unless the teacher understands the human condition, is able to develop and maintain an effective relationship with students, and has a carefully developed theory concerning the place of formal learning in the contemporary world and the place of the teacher in the process of formal learning.

While there are many possible ways of setting forth the crucial questions facing schools of education with respect to teacher education, the foregoing discussion suggests the nature of those questions. How do we prepare teachers capable of helping children to function effectively in a highly technical society, while at the same time acquainting them with their place in Western civilization? How can a concern for humane values be maintained in a society that values efficiency and effectiveness? How can the requirements of bureaucratic organizations be reconciled with the democratic values of individual choice and freedom? How are these concerns related to the process and content of teacher education? What is most fundamental and essential to effective teaching? Special interest groups are pressing legislators to pass bills requiring every teacher to complete courses in conservation, parenting, the effective use of media, the free enterprise system, fundamentals of our legal system, safety and health, and a host of others. Most of these are useful, but are they fundamental for teachers? Given that public research universities include a large collection of scholars interested in just about every conceivable area of knowledge, they are ideal settings for the examination of fundamental issues pertaining to education. Research facilities are substantial. If better answers are to be found to the challenges facing education, the public research university would seem to be a major source of help.

There is at least one important caveat, however. Universities can isolate themselves from the surrounding society. Or perhaps it is more accurate to say that individuals working in universities can isolate themselves. While some educational problems can be explored very successfully apart from practice, in general the essence of educational concerns is focused in practice, in the procedure of educating. In the years immediately ahead more effective approaches to wedding research and practice must be developed. Significant progress has been made in the last decade, and it has been clearly demonstrated that practitioners and university faculty can work together very successfully. A report by Gene Maecoff issued by the Carnegie Foundation for the Advancement of Teaching, *School and College: Partnership in Education*,[2] suggests what can be done in this area. Schools of education in public universities must continually strive to develop the relationships between the agencies that employ their graduates or utilize their research and development products and the university faculty and staff. Schools of agriculture have been very successful in wedding research, training, and practice. Schools of education must now find ways to accomplish this more effectively.

THE NEED FOR RESOURCES

In the last two decades the management of higher education has increasingly been dominated by what are often described as rational procedures. The systems analysts have arrived, replete with their funding formulas, calculation of cost per credit, enrollment projections, faculty work loads, and other numerical techniques for determining who gets what share of the available resources. Traditionally, university administrators have assumed that professional education courses and programs are relatively cheap. Indeed, their inexpensiveness is one of the reasons they exist at more than 1,300 colleges and universities. When formulas began to be developed as a basis for distributing resources to instructional programs, professional education programs were included with the social sciences. Departments such as history; sociology, and economics in large state universities typically include many lecture courses with enrollments of several hundred each at the undergraduate level. They are usually the least expensive instructional programs per credit hour produced in the entire campus. It has been assumed then that if education is a part of the social sciences, it should have comparable costs.

The problem, of course, is that while education derives much of its content and methodology from the social sciences, class size and teaching methodology are quite different. A few courses in educational foundations can be taught as large lectures with costs per pupil comparable with beginning courses in the social sciences. However, most programs in professional education include a large clinical component that requires a relatively low student-faculty ratio. Advanced work in fields such as counseling or the teaching of reading demands very intensive one-on-one diagnostic fieldwork and several hours weekly of faculty supervision of each student. This is one of the most labor-intensive instructional situations found in a university, but existing funding formulas usually are based on quite different assumptions.

In addition, schools of education must now provide students experience in the use of a wide variety of technological aids to the teaching-learning process. Contemporary audio, video, and computer equipment requires a substantial capital budget and a technical support staff not traditionally found in schools of education. The university administration has assumed that schools of engineering, medicine, and agriculture require large capital budgets and specialized nonteaching staff, but not so schools of education. But if the technology that is now a part of learning systems being used in business, industry, and the better-equipped elementary and secondary schools is not also used in schools of education, graduates of schools of education will be ill-prepared to function effectively as educators.

One of the most crucial challenges facing schools of education in public universities is keeping abreast of rapidly changing technology applicable to the teaching-learning process. Without that technology, neither the research programs nor the instructional programs will be relevant to the teaching-learning process being utilized outside universities. This is not a problem just for schools of education, of course. Very substantial increases in the resource base of universities must occur in the next few years if they are to keep pace with the rapid growth of technology. If universities become technologically obsolete, they will become arcane relics of quite limited value. The same can be said of schools of education.

It is relatively easy to imagine the federal government and the several states contributing substantial sums to maintain the effectiveness of university programs in the physical sciences, agriculture, medicine, and engineering. The prospects for schools of education, however, are not so promising. The traditionally low value placed on teachers and teaching has been reinforced in recent years by the belief that the quality of the public schools has deteriorated and that teachers now are generally less able than their predecessors. It will require substantial efforts to convince legislators and the public that additional resources are required to provide teachers the type of training they now need to be effective.

Schools of education in public universities are caught in a difficult trap with respect to resources. Historically, they taught large numbers of students with meager resources, particularly during the period of burgeoning enrollments in higher education following World War II when the teacher shortage encouraged many young people to choose education majors. Schools of education coped as best they could, accepting large enrollment increases without receiving corresponding increases in faculty, capital, and supplies. At about the time when enrollments peaked, the systems analysts began developing funding formulas based on the previous decade's data. As a result, schools of education were assigned, in many cases, very unfavorable resource allocations relative to the rest of the university.

If that were not bad enough, two other developments exacerbated the situation. Teacher shortages turned to teacher surpluses during the 1970s, and in the early 1980s the microcomputer became widely used in elementary and secondary schools. Enrollments in many schools of education fell by as much as 50 percent, but the resources required to provide a quality program increased. Funding formulas, unfortunately, dictated that if you lose students, you lose budget. Individual states, hard-pressed to maintain their expanded system of higher education in the midst of the most serious economic depression since the 1930s, quite naturally looked for those programs with declining enrollments as programs that could be cut. In many cases, this has meant looking at the schools of education.

The damage that has been done by this sequence of developments has been severe and will have long-term consequences. The schools of education in a few large state universities will perhaps not recover, or at least not for many years. Their basic character and form have been fundamentally altered by budget, staff, and program cuts. For most, the consequences will probably be only temporary, a reminder that public universities are vulnerable to economic, political, and demographic changes.

As this is written, there are encouraging signs. Influential people are beginning to speak out on the need to support teacher education and the schools. There is a recognition that what is now needed are positive steps to deal with the weaknesses that have been documented. It will require skilled leadership on the part of schools of education to translate this support into the resources needed to maintain quality programs in the very competitive world of higher education.

THE FACULTY AND PROGRAM QUALITY

An educational program cannot rise above the quality of the individuals who staff it. The single most important task of the faculty of a school of education is selecting colleagues. When a search is under way, every effort should be made to locate individuals more able than present faculty members. Fear of excellence sounds the death knell for any educational institution.

Unfortunately, higher education generally is entering a period in which the quality of applicants for faculty positions is likely to be lower than it has been for several decades. This is even more apt to be true for schools of education. Salaries are mediocre, prestige and status are down, and job security is uncertain. The best and the brightest are more likely to pursue graduate study in other professions or to complete the Ph.D. and go immediately into business or industry where salaries are substantially above those paid by universities.

There are, of course, many more public universities with schools of education now than thirty years ago. Many formerly small state colleges are now large state universities. Consequently, the shrinking pool of potentially high-quality faculty will be spread very thinly among the existing institutions. In addition, just as there are too many colleges and universities preparing teachers, so too are there far too many now approved to offer the doctorate in education while lacking the resources needed to provide a quality graduate program. Is there anything to be done about this situation?

Individual universities or departments do have options. One is to be flexible about credentials while focusing on the intellectual capacities of candidates. We learned in the 1950s and 1960s that persons trained in another discipline but interested enough in education to accept an appointment in a school of education usually drifted back, if they could, to the department of their primary discipline. Perhaps it was a matter of status; perhaps it was just too complicated to be in two departments. For whatever reasons, it did occur very frequently. Hiring a sociologist or psychologist who is willing to give education a try probably will not be much help. But defining the selection criteria for faculty positions rather broadly without giving up on certain essential ones—intelligence, productivity, interest in educational questions—may be of some help.

Perhaps the most important thing is to be aware of the problem so that each search for faculty becomes a special challenge to beat the odds rather than just another routine chore of bringing in a few people for interviews and finding someone who will accept an offer. We must accept the fact that too few able young people are pursuing doctorates in education, and we must set our standards well above the median of the available pool if we are to maintain or enhance overall faculty quality.

Another option involves recognizing the wisdom of reductions. Following World War II schools of education in the large state universities tended to expand their programs very substantially. They now typically offer hundreds of courses and dozens of programs or majors. If quality faculty are scarce and resources inadequate, wisdom suggests reducing courses and programs so that quality can be maintained. A strong faculty in one area of specialization will tend to attract other strong faculty. While it may be possible to replace a faculty member leaving a program or staff judged to be weak, the probability is high that the replacement will be mediocre. We would all do well to examine our programs with candor and admit those areas in which we are weak, particularly at the graduate level. The field of education will be better served if there are a few strong persons preparing doctorates with high-quality faculty clustered in those programs.

POLITICS

Ideally, a dean of a school of education in a public university should have expertise as a classroom teacher, a school administrator, and a university faculty member, as well as be a recognized scholar in some area of research, have a law degree, and have several years' experience in the state legislature. Being successful in business would be helpful in some quarters, too! This list suggests how complex the role of dean has become and how the list of the dean's "significant others" has grown in recent years. The support of legislators is crucial for anyone working in a public university, and legislators are responsive to constituents concerned about education. Teachers, administrators, school boards, business organizations, and citizen groups are now adept at utilizing the political process to influence public schools of education.

The political nature of the education profession itself is as important as the political realities of state government. Rather than being a unified professional group, working in concert for generally accepted goals, professional educators are a complex of competing factions and overlapping special interests. Teacher organizations, which often take the form of teacher unions, are the most significant development in organized labor in the United States over the last two decades. The influence of such groups at all educational levels and in state and federal government has been very substantial and is a permanent part of the educational scene.

During the years when teachers have been organizing, state departments of public instruction have been gaining in power and resources. They now wield much more influence over the schools and universities than in any period in their history, and they are frequently a vehicle for legislative influence. State legislators have begun to take seriously their constitutional right to guide the schools and universities of the state. What university faculty may see as interference and a trampling of faculty prerogatives, legislators see as exercising the will of those who are footing the bill.

In an era dominated by special interest groups and single-issue politics, schools of education are receiving close attention from many quarters. The classrooms of the nation are a key arena in the battle for the minds and values of children; schools of education, which prepare the personnel who staff the schools, are inevitably drawn into the struggle. In contrast, private schools of education are frequently established for the express purpose of preparing teachers committed to the values and perspectives of a particular special interest group. It will require political skill and awareness as well as a commitment to the best traditions of public higher education for schools of education to maintain their integrity and objectivity in the present circumstances.

Historically, public education has been influenced by a succession of fads, some of which addressed demonstrated needs or problems but many of which were pointless or silly or, on occasion, even harmful. Many school facilities built according to the open-classroom fad of the 1960s have now added the walls that were thought to be unnecessary. "New math" has been succeeded by the "newer but mostly old" math. Dozens of such examples could be listed. To what extent should or can schools of education in public universities resist such short-lived movements in favor of more credible but unpopular or unrecognized theories and practices? Dare we ignore the popular clamor, often encouraged by the media, for this or that fad when we know that legislators typically respond strongly to the wishes of the public? We should have learned by now that crash programs, a few conferences, or a piece of legislation do not deal effectively with the needs of the schools.

If schools of education are to provide effective support to the educational system of the country, what choices do they make? Do they attempt to be responsive to the winds of popular opinion and in tune with every fad, or do they conduct the research and training activities that will in the long term strengthen our system of education? Can we develop the credibility needed to maintain our resource base when we believe we must be out of step with the public and the media? Is it necessary for us to engage in a certain amount of game playing, to be political, in response to the shifting public clamor, even while we maintain a steady course pursuing the objectives we believe to be the correct ones?

That final question raises the issue of who does decide for the nation and the profession what are the correct objectives to pursue. As a nation we are confused as to the purposes of schooling, leaving teachers and administrators in doubt as to what we really expect of them. More than ever, we need to recognize the place of the three traditional aims of education—preparation for citizenship, for work, and for personal development—and to formulate an educational program suited to foster all three. While faculty in public universities are not in a position to decide this matter for everyone else, surely they can contribute significantly to the public debate. They should be joined in this effort by teachers and other segments of the education profession.

Schools of education in public universities must begin to play a

more active role in the political dimensions of education. This requires a set of skills and attention to events that have typically not
been of concern to many faculty in those institutions.

THE FUTURE

The consequences of the recent loss of resources by many schools of
education I noted earlier will probably be only temporary. This
judgment may well be too optimistic. If nothing else, the last decade
has proven beyond doubt the vulnerability of professional education
programs in public universities. While riding out the storm may be
difficult, succeeding at that will not be enough. Aggressive, positive
action to improve the image and the reality of schools of education is
essential. This will not be easy, but many of the elements needed
already exist.

Despite recent criticism and the interest of a few in "deschooling"
society, formal education is an absolute essential, given the nature of
our economy and society. Teachers and other educational personnel
are needed and that need will not diminish, although the types of
personnel and their functions may change.

There is a need not only to strengthen ourselves as individual
schools but also to recognize both the vital place of education in the
society and the need for all elements supportive of the total educational system to move together to raise the general effectiveness of the
enterprise. While education in this country includes some large
bureaucracies, it is not monolithic but very complex. There is no one
button to push, no single administrative structure to affect, that will
produce change in the desired direction. Local and state control
remain significant; change on a national scale requires moving a very
complex educational system that does not really function as a system
at all. Public universities are an important element in this system, and
they must help shape a coherent response to the educational needs of
the nation. At present, we lack a national consensus even on the goals
of formal education. Schools of education have a unique place in the
educational system; while our specific mission is to provide educational programs at the undergraduate and graduate level, we also are
closely associated with elementary and secondary schools. Historically, we have prided ourselves in not having a monolithic national

system of education. We must now give close attention to how public universities can be a positive factor in making that system, such as it is, work for all the people of this nation.

The tools required to respond effectively to needs are, in large part, available. In the last two decades research related to pedagogical questions has produced more significant results than ever before. While the total research effort falls far short of what is needed, there is nevertheless a large national educational research community that provides a base for greater effort and productivity in the future. There is a cohort of able faculty trained as specialists in various aspects of the total education enterprise. Training programs incorporating a carefully orchestrated combination of field experiences and theoretical study are in place and demonstrating their value. Cooperative relationships between school-based personnel and academic scholars have been developed that are mutually beneficial and foster the applied research needed to improve practice. Much greater attention is now being given to the nonschool educational programs found in business, industry, hospitals, and other institutions. Schools of education have finally recognized that elementary and secondary schools designed for the young incorporate only a fraction of the total educational enterprise.

The challenge of the immediate future then is to restructure schools of education by responding to these new developments and new potentialities. We need not—indeed, we dare not—stay with the status quo. This will mean different things to different people, and universities will respond differently depending on their current strengths and their histories. It will be unfortunate if schools of education in large state universities fail to take advantage of their institutional setting. They should attempt to define what they can do well and how they can benefit from cooperative relationships with the other units in the university. A school of education should not be a self-contained unit but should utilize the research and instructional programs of other campus units to supplement its own.

Even though the media and many critics of education have incorrectly stated that better teachers will solve all the problems of public education, it is obvious that the children, the schools, and the social conditions demand teachers different from those schools of education have typically been producing. Despite the efforts that have been made since the 1960s, the education of children living in urban ghettos remains a failure save for a few notable exceptions. The challenges presented by mainstreaming have been experienced by most teachers, but the successes have been too few. Greater attention must be given to identifying the needs of special students and how to cope with these needs. For far too many young people high school is not a significant, positive educational experience. But beyond that, one has the sense that the place of formal schooling in the life of both children and adults has changed from what it was even a half-century ago. Our life experiences are qualitatively different because of changes in such fundamental influences as the media, the nature of work, the family, and the community. We have given only fleeting attention to how these changes may affect the character of teaching, learning, and the processes of schooling. This fact should define a large part of the research agenda for schools of education as well as speak clearly to the need for fundamental changes in training programs.

Fortunately, we are moving from condemnation and criticism of education at all levels to a search for solutions. The search tends to point in two different directions—calls for fundamental changes in various facets of education including teacher education or admonitions to do essentially what we are now doing but to do it much better. The words *excellence* and *quality* dominate most discussions, but there is little consensus yet on what they mean or how to reach them. Do we simply need to improve, or must we discard much that we have and replace it with new programs, processes, and institutions?

NOTES

1. See B. O. Smith, *A Design for a School of Pedagogy* (Washington, D.C.: U.S. Government Printing Office, 1980).
2. See Gene I. Maecoff, *School and College: Partnership in Education* (Princeton, N.J.: Carnegie Foundation for the Advancement of Teaching, 1983).

4

Colleges of Education in Urban Universities

Jay D. Scribner

> It was not difficult to supply such a crying
> need . . . to advance education to the masses
> who could not afford to attend school regu-
> larly after they reached earning age.
> — Russel H. Conwell, founder of
> Temple University, in
> *The Angel's Lily* (1920)

Colleges of education have undergone profound changes over the course of this century, but none so dramatic as the recent shift from expansion to decline. In many regions of the country the change has been reflected in falling enrollments, but an even more unpleasant reality has been the national decline in institutional and public support for colleges of education.[1] The problems concomitant with decreasing support have been exacerbated in the large urban university. This chapter addresses these problems.

To understand the mission of the college of education in an urban environment, one must first appreciate what is meant by the *urban perspective*. Thus, it is necessary to provide a brief sketch of the context and evolution of urban universities, then to examine the transformation of colleges of education from an era of unremitting growth and support to the edge of uncertainty, and finally to offer some suggestions for moving beyond survival strategies of the past few decades. First, let us seek an understanding of why urban universities stand apart from institutions of higher education situated in different environments.

THE URBAN PERSPECTIVE

To be called *urban*, a university must be located in a city; however, location is no guarantee of "true urbanism." A truly urban university is one in which the primary focus is to extend formal education to the working classes and to establish ties to urban business, manufacturing, and industrial enterprises. Professional schools and advanced studies in vocational areas are often at the core of instruction, with the arts, humanities, and sciences supporting these career-oriented curricula. In sum, the urban university reflects an "ideal," characterized by incompatible truths, inherent value conflicts, and common concerns for urban life.[2]

Origins of the Urban Perspective

The urban perspective derives from a university tradition in America that is distinctly different from that of Europe. For instance, European universities were initially established in metropolitan cities such as Paris, Berlin, London, and Bologna, drawing students not only from the city but from throughout the Western world. These universities were under pressure to attract gifted scholars, to serve the city, and, above all, to remain as free from controversy as possible.[3] Battles between town and gown and lynchings and punishments meted out for perceived disloyalty, independence of thought, and simply lecturing elsewhere all led to what the professorial ranks of today most jealousy protect—academic freedom.[4] This preciously guarded virtue of higher education was fought for—and won—in the city.

Unlike European universities, institutions of higher learning in this country were founded basically on rural soil, outside the city. In 1636 Boston followed London's experience with Oxford and Cambridge, as Harvard College sought refuge outside the more populous center of commerce, literature, and art. By contrast, established cities in Europe sought university leadership in the economic and intellectual areas of the city. With more settlements than cities in America, the first colleges were established primarily to provide a liberal arts education—knowledge for its own sake—to an educated clergy.[5] Harvard, Yale, Princeton, and a small group of other pre-Revolutionary War universities purposively avoided the distractions of the cities.

Moreover, during the postcolonial period of the late eighteenth century, and throughout the nineteenth century, several private universities, including Temple University, the University of Pittsburgh, New York University, and Western Reserve University, were formed—usually, but not always—on the edge of the city. Unlike their earlier counterparts, these institutions began to establish special missions relevant and responsive to urban needs.[6]

Private denominational schools, for the most part, sought the solitude of the quiet villages and small towns of America. Catholic universities, particularly those run by Jesuits, were exceptions; these were more likely to be located in an urban environment because the Catholic population tended to settle in the cities. And because of the rapid industrial development in America, technical schools such as Carnegie Institute of Technology, Case Institute, and the Massachusetts Institute of Technology, which were all closely tied to America's expanding horizons in science and technology during the early part of the twentieth century, were each located within or close to an urban setting.[7]

Public institutions of higher education in America date back to the nineteenth century. Municipal universities, followed by state land-grant schools, were established for reasons other than religious or exclusively personal benefits for the elite.[8] From the beginning, public institutions of higher learning were standard bearers for egalitarianism and social purpose. Opening their doors to the common man, these institutions attempted to improve America's productivity in agriculture in the rural areas and in industry, manufacturing, and commerce in the cities.

These vocation- and service-oriented schools hired as faculty many Americans who had returned to the United States in the final decades of the nineteenth century after studying at the universities of Berlin, Hamburg, and Frankfurt; thus, public higher education became influenced by German educational concepts.[9] This influence derived from a form of elitism, but an elitism more pragmatic than the English or French versions in which education, pursued for its own sake, was available only to develop morally superior males. Thus, the public higher education institution in America encouraged study in graduate education, research, and the applied sciences in addition to offering a basic service and vocational orientation.[10]

In sum, the special character of the urban university may be seen most by its gaze toward social responsibility. The large urban multiversity with its multiple missions will behave differently from those institutions primarily concerned with imparting and producing knowledge. As Henry Commager puts it:

> If our universities are to enjoy the advantages of their urban position, if they are to be to American society what the great urban universities of Europe have been to their societies, they must assume responsibility for the development of urban and regional civilization.[11]

By their very nature, American universities cultivate fertile ground for value conflicts over purpose and program goals. For urban universities these conflicts intensify, not only because of the unique history of these schools, but also because of their diverse constituencies, the proximity of their clients, and the constantly changing demands for priorities and programs to meet urban needs.

Some Contradictions and Dilemmas

As part of the urban university, the college of education is pressed to respond to the same challenges. Franklin Spikes mentions four paradoxes found in institutions of higher learning, particularly in urban universities: elitism versus egalitarianism, quality versus quantity, institutional versus individual influence, and professionalism versus humanism.[12] Each paradox engenders debate and determines policy. Each paradox also either facilitates or inhibits the extent to which a college of education gains support and leverage within an urban university to answer to its responsibility of meeting the educational needs of an urban environment.

Colleges of education began as one-year, then later became two-year normal schools for teacher training. They subsequently evolved into three-year and then four-year colleges. Until recently, departments, schools, and colleges of education emphasized concepts of schooling—

with particular concentration on elementary and secondary levels of public education—rather than efforts to explore and resolve problems of human learning in a large societal context.[13] As new roles emerged in the administration of schools, such as staff supervision, student counseling, program evaluation and bilingual education, a plethora of subspecializations, departmental programs, and required and elective courses appeared in college curriculum bulletins and catalogues.

Historically, colleges of education have often been the subject of criticism. In this, they have not been an exception. No school or college on the typical university campus has evolved without becoming fragmented, specialized, and uneven in the quality of teaching, research, and service. This is particularly evident on campuses where conflicts exist between the purists and the interdisciplinarians, and between those who support scholarship that seems to have no immediate applicability and those who encourage scholarship that can immediately be applied to contemporary social problems. Because of their unstinting investment in solving problems of the urban communities, conflict over mission tends to occur most frequently in urban universities.[14]

David Clark and Egon Guba conclude that the college of education in the urban university, "which attempted to solve the community's educational problems with a handful of staff originally employed to teach classes for undergraduate and graduate classes," sets the most trenchant example of mission overreach.[15] The most widely shared mission of colleges of education is teacher training;[16] few of them consider research a primary purpose. However, in many instances during the rapid expansion of colleges of education in the 1960s and early 1970s, their missions diversified and their goals multiplied. Their objectives were found to be incongruent with faculty strength, base of fiscal support, and general environment,[17] particularly when faculty denied they had a responsibility to solve urban educational problems, to eradicate institutional racism, and to prepare students to fulfill vital educational roles in the urban community.

Like schools of social work and preparatory programs for the clergy, colleges of education traditionally—and ideally—have attempted to build a gateway to a better life for the urban poor. This concept has held strong throughout the twentieth century. Historically, however, the more common practice in higher education has been to exclude systematically the urban poor.[18] While a few students attending colleges of education earlier in this century assumed careers in the "common schools," the majority of working or welfare poor rarely saw higher education as an avenue for upward mobility.[19] More significantly, institutional policies in regard to entrance requirements and scholarships for "charity students" often discriminated against children of the urban poor. Even the free municipal universities favored the more affluent students.[20] As recently as 1978, Berube reported:

> Few public urban universities have succeeded in grappling with the problems of educating the urban poor. A major study of accessible higher education . . . disclosed a haphazard educational pattern that unconsciously neglected the urban poor. Approximately three-fourths of our major urban centers are markedly lacking in available colleges and universities that provide a measure of free access, defined as institutions where it is relatively easy to be admitted and that maintain free or low-cost tuition.[21]

Even though urban universities espouse egalitarian values, elitist concepts have had considerable impact on programs and policies of their schools and colleges. With few exceptions, boards of trustees are dominated by the upper crust of the urban community, and faculty senates often are populated with traditionalists from the arts and sciences. Consequently, colleges of education are often engaged in disputes between undergraduate and graduate faculties and between social research and professionally oriented groups. For example, access to higher education is a dividing issue; some educators favor flexible entrance requirements (typically for the larger populations of black and Hispanic students), while others argue for higher entrance standards, believing that intelligence, grades, and SAT scores predict success.

To adopt an *urban perspective*, one must accept the inconsistencies that pervade institutions of higher learning, while at the same time remembering—and believing in—the origins of the urban university, an institution that set out to improve life for everyone in the community. Established to fulfill special needs and to resolve educational problems in meeting them, colleges of education, unlike other "professional" schools, made it possible for countless numbers of the urban poor, as well as the working class, to become role models for generations of young people striving for upward mobility.

Therein lies the dilemma of the urban university. As Spikes so aptly acknowledges:

> There often is a thin line between elitism and pride, and the latter is necessary for the internal health of any institution. To feel entirely "unspecial" is to lose all hope. Ironically, to be genuinely egalitarian in this society is to be really very special—but too few people have an elementary understanding of this fact.[22]

UNREMITTING GROWTH TO THE EDGE OF UNCERTAINTY

Enjoying a most privileged status in American society for the past twenty years, urban universities successfully trained students to meet head-on the challenges to make urban life better for everyone, greatly aided by fiscal support for this mission. Until the neoconservative wave swept over the country in the mid-1970s, colleges of education assumed the major responsibility, thrust on them by federal, state, and local educational agencies, to provide leadership in turning the urban educational system around.

In recent years, however, colleges of education have been pushed to the brink of uncertainty. Caught in a virtual whipsaw of pressures, they have come under increasingly close scrutiny by both the larger university community and the ubiquitous self-examination process of the education profession. On the one side, there has been a shift away from a commitment to expansionism, social responsibility, and governmental intervention and toward supply-side economics, tax cuts, decreases in federal spending, tightening budgets, and balancing the bottom line. This shift has had a significant impact on programs, morale, and efficiency. On the other side, a sluggish and inflationary economy and a sharp decline in the college-age population have triggered a fear of imminent disaster for urban universities.[23]

Neoconservative critics have reacted with cynicism to those urban universities that fueled and supported liberal movements, tolerated Vietnam War protesters, and provided a haven for humanists who offered alternative educational programs to blacks, Hispanics, and the working-class poor. Disaffection with the New Frontier and Great Society movements, with their racial integration, affirmative action, equal opportunity, and war-on-poverty programs, pervades the social, economic, and political landscape of the 1980s. There is no question that the public mood has drifted rightward in recent times. To understand the consequences of this change and the challenges for colleges of education in the future, the following three scenarios depicting the past, present, and future are presented.

Scenario I. The Past: Managing by Addition

During the past two decades, and until only recently, educational institutions at all levels were managed with a go-go style of enthusiasm and devil-take-the-hindmost attitude. University presidents hired deans because of their reputations as agents of change and their sensitivity toward the urban mission. Deans, in turn, hired department chairpersons, associate deans, division heads, and others because of their experience in curricular reforms, interest in pursuing educational policy studies, and propensity toward encouraging interdisciplinary problem-solving and training projects involving collaboration among the university, the community, and the school district. Between ten and twenty new faculty members were hired per year in the late 1960s and early 1970s by colleges of education in large urban universities.[24]

Change during this period was inevitable, and not particularly managed. Unquestionably, the objective observer can identify ad infinitum dramatic changes in delivery systems, program development, course content, social and political attitudes, student populations, and notions about meritocracy. The rapid growth created the illusion that educational institutions were effective—an illusion that often proved more useful than real.

With their many grants, the influx of "new" students, and their sights on ameliorating educational opportunities in the urban neighborhoods, colleges of education forged recognition, pride, and a sense of power on urban campuses and were envied, encouraged, assailed, and applauded by faculty and administration.

Then the mood changed. An unpopular war whose losses were recorded like a daily Dow Jones report galvanized students. An advanced technology came under public scrutiny as its voracious appetite for natural resources became a source of discontent. Diminishing supplies of energy and raw materials, the persistence of poverty, the plight of the cities, and the challenges of those excluded from the mainstream because of race and/or social standing in society were among the forces contributing to a cataclysmic change of mood not only in society, but also on the campus. Moreover, declining birth rates, job opportunities, and mobility and the inability of higher education to solve these and related urban problems quickly added to the trend toward devaluating the social importance of higher education. Nonetheless, inflated egos and puffy self-esteem often carried faculty and administrators of colleges of education through these troubled and turbulent times.

During this era of management by addition, new attitudes, skills, and know-how for coping with growth were developed. As a gateway to not only national but also personal fulfillment, the path to economic growth was eagerly followed. Continuous growth in the country's population, in per capita real income, and in the gross national product—despite coming under attack in the mid-1960s by anticapitalists, socialists, and ecologists—continued unremittingly to be a national goal. Between 1950 and 1970 unprecedented numbers of college applicants were accommodated by the expansion policies of governments.[25] However, the results of these state and local policies have proved costly in the 1980s.[26]

Scenario II. The Present: Managing Decline

Contrast my brief interpretation of the past with the present picture. A declining demographic pattern, which projects over the next fifteen years a decrease at a national rate of 25 percent in the number of traditional college-age students, concerns all constituencies both within and outside the urban university. In large metropolitan areas the decline in enrollment is projected at 40 to 50 percent.[27] The southeast, south central, and western states appear to be declining in projected 18-year-old populations at a far lesser rate than the rest of the country. Urban universities feel the economic pinch most acutely, but it should be noted that no region completely escapes the burdens brought about by falling enrollments.

In addition, the nation's economy is slowly surrendering its preeminence in industrial production and annual growth rate to other countries, notably West Germany and Japan.[28] Moreover, the world-wide use of computers, robotics, and sophisticated communication satellites has contributed to weakening America's previously strong—and unquestioned—leadership in the world marketplace. Because of a growing interdependence among countries in the manufacturing of goods and in commercial trade, enormous pressure has been placed on our nation to maximize profits from the exportation of products and ideas. Colleges of education are facing the same economic challenges. The well-lined purse of the 1960s has been replaced by hand-to-mouth subsistence. With alarming swiftness, public support in the form of revenue is drying up, and, thus,deficits are abounding, making it extremely difficult to upgrade laboratories, acquire the latest scientific technology, and improve the physical environment of campuses. The struggle becomes one of how to respond to changing expectations and new demands with limited, even diminishing, resources.

The political climate, likewise, is changing. Political action committees and single-interest groups are wielding increasing power and influence, thereby weakening the core of both major political parties. The neoconservative movement led to a major political realignment of the Republican party and landslide victories for President Reagan in 1980 and 1984. Voters expressed disdain for big government, big bureaucracy, and high taxes; some political observers suggested that the very success of the Democrats in fostering big government intervention over the years ultimately pushed them out of office. The "have not," inner-city, blue-collar workers of the earlier period of this century raised their socioeconomic status, becoming middle-class suburbanites, and then, in turn, voted against spending to assist today's urban poor and urban programs.[29]

Thus, with this perspective, presidents of urban universities are calling for balanced budgets, accurate planning data, and new—and viable—marketing strategies. Provosts are asking for redefinition of missions and objectives, for a common curriculum, and for reallocation of resources. Colleges are being urged to cut, consolidate, and trim expenditures, increase faculty productivity, and, above all, pursue excellence in teaching, research, and service. Faculty are seeking ties with business and industry, articulation with technology, and marketing possibilities for new programs. These patterns of interaction suggest a network of strategies aimed at adapting to, as well as resisting, the decline.[30]

The present context of uncertainty for colleges of education in the urban university has given rise to discontent, stress, and anxiety among faculty and students. For faculty, the university has become a battleground in which tenure and academic freedom are under attack from real or implied threats of retrenchment. Moreover, for faculty of professional schools, particularly those in colleges of education, the need for retraining, acquiring new skills, and seeking new visions has never been more acute as society moves inexorably toward a high-technology, information-oriented economy. The National Commission on Excellence in Education has underscored these unprecedented demands for colleges of education in its dramatic report, *A Nation at Risk: The Imperative for Educational Reform.*[31]

Students are discouraged, to say the least. They face a sagging economy; swelling numbers of graduates of liberal arts, education, and social welfare schools are unemployed; they recognize the evolving reality that they cannot now even compete for jobs in fields in which their higher-order mathematics skills, problem-solving abilities, and science training were once in demand. This malevolent economic hammer has hit institutions of higher learning nationwide, but for urban universities with heavily enrolled remediation programs, the problems have struck with even greater weight.[32]

Managing decline involves strategies for resistance that seek new markets, new delivery systems, new products, and new sources of revenue. During a period of expansionism many intended and unintended alternative missions emerged, but *adapting* to decline requires skill in cutting back programs and resources in a manner that will least affect the primary missions. Those who succeed in meeting this challenge will have to adopt a management style that modulates participatory, consultative, and authoritarian approaches to leadership. Those who steer their colleges through the turbulent times of this decade will welcome the future because the lessons learned from the past era of management by addition and the present era of management of decline can only enhance the probability of a successful future for managing change.

Scenario III. The Future: Managing Change

Until now there has been little pressure to alter the basic machinery that makes our universities run. When adding new programs or implementing innovative practices, decisions were made in an atmosphere of ferment and enthusiasm. Making the right judgment was often of less concern than making a decision that would ensure one's institution of "getting a piece of the action." When a wrong decision was made, it could be ignored by simply diverting attention to what did work. However, during the period of decline, when the range of choices narrowed, decisions became more susceptible to public scru-

tiny; thus, making judgments that would affect programs and resources (human and material) became exceedingly more difficult and
critical in determining the future of the university. The survival
slogan read: plan or perish!

Those who led their institutions on a steady course during periods
of expansion and decline did so with great skill, courage, and vision.
Now with an impending need to manage accelerating change, there
are obvious implications for significant reevaluation of old leadership
styles, past values, and obsolete objectives and programs. Coping with
rapid societal change, developing human responses to high technology, and steering a steady course into the future will require not only
adaptive individuals but also adaptive organizations.[33]

Adaptability has not been a highly shared value in institutions of
higher learning. To manage change in the future, then, decision
makers in urban universities will have to consider several factors.
Historically, institutions of higher education have had a stake in the
status quo—the first to argue for change but the last to undertake it.
The occasional demands from clients, community, and government to
change the structure, processes, and operation of colleges and universities appear to have had only superficial impact.[34] Moreover, when a
university governance structure proposed change, seeking to enhance
the efficiency and vitality of an academic operation, what Michael
Cohen and James March have called "organizational anarchy" often
resulted.[35] To manage within such an environment, the distinction
between competence and legitimacy and the person and the position
must be understood. Kenneth Mortimer and T. R. McConnell address this problem:

> Professionals do not feel obliged to respond to the claims of legitimacy made by
> administrators. Likewise, administrators are often frustrated by their inability to
> exercise over professionals the kinds of control that they perceive to be necessary
> for efficient operation. This appears to be a fundamental and persisting problem
> with which organizations employing professionals must live. Conflicting claims to
> legitimacy are never fully sorted out or resolved to the satisfaction of all parties.[36]

In an environment of faculty senates and faculty unions, in which
representatives, consultation, and the horizontal distribution of authority are bywords, and in which the industrial approach is often
diffused with the collegial approach and vice versa, managing change
in the future will be a challenging—and formidable—undertaking.[37]

However, due to the consequences of the recent decline including cutbacks in programs and personnel, faculty generally are now willing to take a more active part in the change process. And that can only facilitate the process of change.

Managing change to alter the future of urban universities in a substantive way will require more than periodic attacks on institutional problems or demagogic threats to those who oppose change. Urban universities will flourish and survive only if those who manage them reach beyond sporadic, disconnected, and expedient approaches to solving their problems.[38] Urban universities will not flourish and survive if those who manage them play upon society's prejudices against ivory towers and eggheads and impugn the credibility of those who seek knowledge for its own sake.

Managing change in colleges of education must involve participation from a broad constituency. The support system must include other professions, disciplines, and colleagues outside the colleges of education, as well as from education practitioners, alumni, and the larger community.[39] Thus, combined with the existing strength of the faculty and students of colleges of education, managers of change will be able to address the short- and long-term needs of not only the educational processes but also the lifelong learning needs of the city.[40] By infusing new values, agents of change will be able to reconfirm the essential mission of urban universities to replace obsolescent goals with new curricula, programs, and pedagogy and, most importantly, with a proactive response to providing new opportunities for upward mobility and success in urban America.

BEYOND SURVIVAL STRATEGIES

Colleges of education in urban universities occupied center stage during the educational reform movement of the 1960s. During the decade that followed, however, their image became somewhat tarnished. As forerunners of the earlier reform movement, colleges of education experimented with new curricula and programs that addressed the problems of urban education. Colleges of education provided the urban poor with access to a quality education and actively participated in outreach opportunities for schools and neighborhoods. Because some of their faculty members were active problem solvers, colleges of education became easy targets in the decade that followed—targets within the university for critics reflecting the elitist values of academia and targets outside the university for critics reflecting the emerging neoconservative values of the larger society. Because colleges of education were the first to experience enrollment decline, doubts were raised about the capacity of these colleges to improve opportunities for the socioeconomic advancement of urban youth.

A new image and a reaffirmation of the traditional role of the urban college of education is sorely needed in the 1980s. Resolution of the long-standing conflict between egalitarian and elitist values will occur only if lessons learned in the three scenarios I have presented result in a willingness to take action, to get things done, to experiment, and to move beyond the survival strategies of the past few decades.

What did we learn from the lesson of disjointed incrementalism during the era of management by addition? To what extent have the coping strategies used during the period of managing decline drawn colleges of education away from their original mission? What can be done about organizational rigidity, and what price will we as individuals pay for resisting new program and policy proposals during the impending era of managing change? The success of strategies employed to make colleges of education a viable force in ameliorating urban educational problems in the 1980s and beyond depends largely on the ability of college leadership, faculty, students, administration, and alumni to learn from, and move beyond, disjointed incrementalism, coping strategies, and organizational rigidity. Positive action will be required to create a vital and dynamic image for colleges of education as institutions committed to the goal of helping urban youngsters to realize their potential and to compete on a basis of equality with other graduates of colleges and universities throughout the country.

Beyond Disjointed Incrementalism

Strategic planning[41] appears to be a viable alternative to disjointed incrementalism, the "shotgun" approach to developing programs for urban education. Strategic planning replaces long-range planning and provides a strategy for survival that many university administrators view as the panacea that will allow for steadiness in troubled times. Because of the unpredictability of environmental and internal factors—for example, the shifting circumstances of the budget, capricious administrative behavior, and the necessarily changing demands of plans themselves—any blueprint for strategic planning that extends five years or more is considered unrealistic.

Victor Baldridge defines strategic planning as

> developing a good fit between the organization's activities and the demands of the environment around it. Strategic planning looks at the big picture—the long-range destiny of the institution, the competition between this organization and others in the environment, the market for organizational products and services, the mix of internal resources to accomplish the organization's purpose. Strategic planning emphasizes flexibility and quick response to changes in the outside environment. . . . It is not so much interested in doing things right, it is more concerned with doing the right things. Effectiveness, not efficiency, is the goal of strategic planning.[42]

As defined, strategic planning involves flexibility, adaptability, and tactical decision making, all of which must be undertaken within a tight and inflexible set of core values. Such core values are those few "oughts" that guide the college or university in making decisions and policies and constitute a frame of reference within which the "urban mission" can be addressed. Thus, strategic planning will flourish in an atmosphere of openness and action in which individuals and groups exchange ideas toward creating, testing, adapting, and changing programs and policies.

What are the three or four core values of the entire university? What is the mission of the college of education? How does the college relate to the community? Does it seek to get its share of the market? Do those making strategic decisions consider the wants, needs, and desires of their constituencies? Is more emphasis placed on effectiveness than efficiency? Are contingencies being developed for a rapidly changing, technologically oriented society? Is proper emphasis placed on short- and medium-range issues? While these ongoing questions seek answers, Baldridge contends that key leaders must engage in "jugular vein" decisions that not only support but also often determine the direction of strategic plans.[43]

Working with their provosts and faculty committees, deans select key faculty to assist in managing change and setting up agenda for the future. However, assembling a high-powered caucus of educators to address and answer the questions raised above does not promise the reality of action unless the university's central administration publicly supports the college of education in its mission to play a vital resource role in the urban community. Following Baldridge's analogy, "jugular vein" decisions require the life support of the "heart" of the university.

Beyond Coping Strategies

Coping strategies were used during the eras of both expansionism and decline. However, when institutional change of a fundamental nature is necessary, coping strategies often fail, and for the same reasons that disjointed incrementalism has been found to be an unsatisfactory decision-making strategy: coping strategies divert an organization away from its intended mission and create a problem of credibility for clients and constituencies.[44]

Coping strategies used by colleges of education in urban universities have been either hailed as responsive to decline or condemned as a departure from institutional missions, goals, and values. Off-campus programs in the suburbs and even farther beyond the metropolis (extending even overseas), weekend courses, minicourses, and all too flexible academic requirements constitute delivery systems in conflict with traditional values. Clearly, some programs, techniques, and policy changes resulting from attempts by colleges of education to resist and adapt to decline have strengthened their urban missions; others have weakened it, and still others have ignored it altogether. Due to organization drift, uncoordinated responses, and the diverse values for which survival strategies are designed, new perspectives are called for on efficiency, productivity, and rationality, as well as a thawing of predetermined biases, prejudices, and assumptions concerning what is legitimate and what is not.

Although the operation of colleges of education, like that of other organizations, involves processes governed by chance alone, leadership is expected to act logically and rationally. In moving beyond survival strategies, leadership must validate management decisions by clarifying its purpose to clients and constituencies, as well as by demonstrating a consensus on mission and legitimacy of programs and policies. It may not be too far-fetched to think of a president, provost, or dean on an urban campus as

a bit like the driver of a skidding automobile. The marginal judgments he makes, his skill, and his luck may possibly make some difference to the survival prospects for his riders. As a result, his responsibilities are heavy. But whether he is convicted of manslaughter or receives a medal for heroism is largely outside his control.[45]

Securing legitimacy, universitywide commitment, and equity in the distribution of resources will mean a more intensive, aggressive approach to running a college than has been practiced in the past. Eight basic findings, distilled from an internal study of the operation of sixty-two companies, offer management guidance to all who share in the leadership of a university.[46] This study, comprising firms associated with high-tech, service, project-managed, resource-based, and consumer and industrial product industries, showed that "excellent companies were, above all, brilliant on the basics."[47] This distinction resulted from employing the following principles:

1. A bias for action
2. Getting close to the customer
3. Autonomy and entrepreneurship
4. Productivity through people
5. Hands-on, value-driven activity
6. Stick to the knitting
7. Simple form, lean staff
8. Simultaneous loose-tight properties.[48]

The lessons learned from this study run counter to uncoordinated strategies for coping with decline. To avoid being paralyzed by decline, leaders of colleges of education will need to embrace "a bias for action," instead of spending an inordinate amount of time analyzing the potential consequences of each decision. Moreover, "getting closer to the customer" will mean not only decisive action on the part of faculty and administrators, but also a clear-cut effort toward improving relations with traditional and nontraditional students, college alumni, and the public. This connection to the customer must elicit information and evaluations that will: (1) improve the quality, type, and range of services offered to our clients, (2) upgrade teaching skills and the different modes of instruction (that is, the new technologies), and (3) conduct decision-oriented research that will benefit the urban community. To accomplish these objectives, leaders of colleges of education must be given the opportunity to divert their attention from the expenditure to the revenue side of the organization.

Those decision makers seeking innovation will find it necessary to review, reinforce, and eliminate obsolete programs and courses that contribute to an overall fragmentation of curricula. Leadership as well as innovation must be encouraged throughout the college; we/they approaches must be discouraged. Deans, department chairs, program heads, and the like must take time to acquaint themselves fully with and understand the changes being pursued not only in their own bailiwick of responsibility, but also throughout the university. Diversity is necessary—but not the kind of willy-nilly diversity that will clearly be a departure from "sticking to the knitting."

Finally, the extent to which coping strategies developed during the era of decline continue to move urban colleges of education away from their mission may be determined by the ability of leadership to implement successfully "simple form, lean staff" and "simultaneous loose-tight properties." For example, how can leaders in colleges of education unravel the complexity in organizational structure to make substantive change possible? How can they begin to intensify the focus on priorities that were diluted by the legion of labyrinthine divisions, departments, and programs? Leadership of the future will have to break old habits, identify core values, establish an open climate anu culture, and provide individuals and groups with an even greater opportunity to respond proactively to the educational needs of the urban community.

Beyond Rigidity

Cataclysmic change or even an accelerating rate of change occasions resistance. For some, coping with change means denying reality. For example, many superintendents of public school systems and presidents of institutions of higher learning often report enrollment figures as either increasing or holding steady, unwilling to admit to a decline. Whether organizations are viewed as radical or reactionary will not matter when change comes; ultimately, they will operate between conservative parameters. Richard Hall argues:

> In education, schools in urban areas have seen their constituencies change around them, but there is a strong tendency toward maintenance of the educational programs that were appropriate in the past, despite their growing irrelevance— and the same change could be documented in higher education.[49]

The ongoing conflict between values adopted in medieval times and new values to meet the demands of contemporary society indicate that conservatism is still healthy in our institutions of higher education. In his examination of the university's many ethical and social responsibilities, Derek Bok contends that responsibility "exists quite distinct from the vision produced either by traditionalists or by social activists."[50] Further, he asserts:

> Those who hold this position recognize that universities have an obligation to serve society by making the contributions they are uniquely able to provide. In carrying out this duty, everyone concerned must try to take account of many different values—the preservation of academic freedom, the maintenance of high intellectual standards, the protection of academic pursuits from outside interference, the rights of individuals affected by the university not to be harmed in their legitimate interests, the needs of those who stand to benefit from the intellectual services that a vigorous university can perform. The difficult task that confronts all academic leaders is to decide how their institution can respond to important social problems in a manner that respects all of these important interests.[51]

Thus, overcoming tradition and rigid conformity to past values, norms, and behavior will require a capacity for self-renewal, redefining missions, reordering priorities, and creative commingling of agendas for action. We must foster an atmosphere in which both compassion and realism interface, and in which new ideas are not only welcome but also encouraged. However, there is an inherent danger in maintaining this perspective. Historically, the higher education community, as it matures with change, tends to narrow its ideas, responses, options, and vision and to restrict its independent thought. Overcoming rigidity, then, will mean a constant development of new experiences for faculty, new organizational matrices for "getting things done" in the urban environment, and new attitudes toward leadership, responsibility, and accountability. The future begins now.

NOTES

1. For evidence supporting this assertion, see David W. Breneman, *The Coming Enrollment Crises* (Washington, D.C.: Association of Governing Boards of Universities and Colleges, 1982); Harry Judge, *American Graduate Schools of Education: A View from Abroad* (New York: Ford Foundation, 1982); and the 1983 reports of the Commission on Excellence in Education, the Twentieth Century Fund's Task Force on Federal Elementary and Secondary Educational Policy, and the National Task Force on Economic Growth.

2. Maurice R. Berube, *The Urban University in America* (Westport, Conn.: Greenwood Press, 1978), p. 14.
3. J. Martin Klotsche, *The Urban University and the Future of Our Cities* (New York: Harper & Row, 1966), p. 2.
4. Ibid., pp. 2-3.
5. Clark Kerr, *The Uses of the University* (New York: Harper & Row, 1966), p. 12.
6. Klotsche, *Urban University,*
7. Ibid., pp. 9-10.
8. William S. Carlson, *The Municipal University* (Washington, D.C.: Center for Applied Research in Education, 1962), pp. 4-6.
9. Kermit C. Parsons, "A Truce in the War Between Universities and Cities," *Journal of Higher Education* 34 (January 1963):18, 21.
10. Kerr, *Uses of the University,* pp. 11-15.
11. Henry Steele Commager, "Is Ivy Necessary?" *Saturday Review,* September 17, 1960, p. 89; cited in Klotsche, *Urban University,* p. 22.
12. W. Franklin Spikes, *The University and the Inner City* (Lexington, Mass.: Lexington Books, 1980), pp. 3-7.
13. Herman Niebuhr, Jr., "Strengthening the Human Learning System," *Change* 14 (November-December 1982): 16-21.
14. George Nash, *The University and the City: Eight Cases of Involvement* (New York: McGraw-Hill, 1973), pp. 3-6.
15. David Clark and Egon Guba, "Schools, Colleges, and Departments of Education: Demographic and Contextual Features," in *The Dilemma of the Deanship,* edited by Daniel Griffiths and Donald McCarty (Danville, Ill.: Interstate, 1980), pp. 79-80.
16. Ibid., p. 80.
17. Ibid.
18. Berube, *Urban University in America,* p. 23.
19. Ibid., p. 24.
20. Only the affluent could afford to go to college. The only exceptions were "charity students" who were bright enough to get a scholarship. When free schools came on the scene, neither the working poor nor the welfare poor had access to them.
21. Berube, *Urban University in America,* p. 26.
22. Spikes, *University and the Inner City,* p. 4.
23. For many universities endowments and gifts to the university are less than 10 percent of their total revenue. This, of course, reflects social class differences between those who attend the various types of institutions of higher education.
24. See Breneman, *Coming Enrollment Crises*; James R. Mingle, *The Challenges of Retrenchment* (San Francisco: Jossey-Bass, 1981).
25. Breneman, *Coming Enrollment Crises,* p. 9.
26. Mingle, *Challenges of Retrenchment,* pp. 2-4.
27. Breneman, *Coming Enrollment Crises,* p. 12.
28. A "new pecking order" in the world economy is discussed in John Naisbitt, *Megatrends* (New York: Warner Books, 1982), pp. 55-77.
29. Walter Isaacson and Evan Thomas, "Running with the PAC's," *Time,* October 25, 1982, p. 20.

30. Mingle, *Challenges of Retrenchment*, ch. 4.
31. National Commission on Excellence in Education, *A Nation at Risk: The Imperative for Educational Reform* (Washington, D.C.: U.S. Department of Education, 1983).
32. Carnegie Council on Policy Studies in Higher Education, *Three Thousand Futures* (San Francisco: Jossey-Bass, 1980), pp. 193-95.
33. Warren G. Bennis and Phillip E. Slater, *The Temporary Society* (New York: Harper & Row, 1963), pp. 106-9.
34. Demands for change that would affect academic freedom or threaten tenure set the stage for confrontation with faculty. See Richard P. Chait and Andrew T. Ford, *Beyond Traditional Tenure* (San Francisco: Jossey-Bass, 1982), ch. 1; Kenneth Mortimer and T. R. McConnell, *Sharing Authority Effectively* (San Francisco: Jossey-Bass, 1978), pp. 161-62; Walter P. Metzger, "Academic Future in America: A Historical Essay," in Commission on Academic Tenure in Higher Education, *Faculty Tenure: A Report and Recommendations* (San Francisco: Jossey-Bass, 1973), p. 3.
35. Michael Cohen and James March, *Leadership and Ambiguity* (New York: McGraw-Hill, 1974), pp. 195-229.
36. Mortimer and McConnell, *Sharing Authority Effectively*, pp. 21-22.
37. J. Victor Baldridge, D. V. Curtis, G. Ecker, and G. L. Riley, eds. *Policy Making and Effective Leadership* (San Francisco: Jossey-Bass, 1978), ch. 4.
38. Bennis and Slater, *Temporary Society*, pp. 83-86.
39. In Baldridge et al., *Policy Making and Effective Leadership*, pp. 45-46, the political interpretation of leadership emphasizes expertise and persuasion rather than "rule with an iron hand." Acquiring constituent support is seen as a political skill of university leaders.
40. Spikes, *University and the Inner City*, pp. 65-69.
41. Marvin W. Peterson, "Analyzing Alternative Approaches to Planning," in *Improving Academic Management: Handbook of Planning and Institutional Research*, edited by Paul Jedamus, Marvin W. Peterson, and associates (San Francisco: Jossey-Bass, 1980), pp. 120-21.
42. J. Victor Baldridge, "Strategic Planning in Higher Education: Does the Emperor Have Any Clothes?" in *The Dynamics of Organizational Change in Education*, edited by J. Victor Baldridge and Terrence Deal (Berkeley: McCutchan Publishing Corp., 1983), p. 173.
43. Ibid., pp. 181-83.
44. See Anthony Downs, "Alternative Futures for the American Ghetto," *Daedalus* 97 (Fall 1968):1331-78. Disjointed incrementalism consists typically of an informal serial attack on social problems. Only a limited number of alternatives and consequences are considered, and objectives and policies are continuously redefined and adjusted to each other throughout the implementation.
45. Michael Cohen and James March, "Leadership in an Organized Anarchy," in *Dynamics of Organizational Change in Education*, p. 340.
46. Thomas J. Peters and Robert H. Waterman, Jr., *In Search of Excellence: Lessons from America's Best-Run Companies* (New York: Harper & Row, 1982), p. 19.
47. Ibid., p. 13.
48. Ibid., pp. 13-16 and chs. 4-12.

49. Richard Hall, *Organizations: Structure and Process* (Englewood Cliffs, N.J.: Prentice-Hall, 1972), p. 343.
50. Derek Bok, *Beyond the Ivory Tower* (Cambridge, Mass.: Harvard University Press, 1982), pp. 87-88.
51. Ibid., p. 88.

Schools of Education and Programs for Continuing Professional Development

Sam J. Yarger, Sally Mertens, and Kenneth R. Howey

It is commonly accepted that employees in most lines of work need training of one sort or another throughout their working years. Currently, there is a press for schools, colleges, and departments of education to address this need for continuing professional development (CPD) of personnel employed in many diverse segments of our nation's work force. Some have argued that schools of education should, in fact, provide the leadership for meeting this pervasive educational need.[1] Historically, schools of education have been involved, to varying degrees, in providing CPD for educational personnel working in schools. This has been accomplished primarily through graduate programs and, to some extent, under the banner of "in-service" training or "staff development." This newly proposed mission is much broader in scope, however, and emphasizes CPD of personnel in such nonschool settings as the military, business, industry, the health professions, and a variety of social services.

Three questions demand serious consideration: (1) Why should schools of education be interested in CPD for nonschool personnel? (2) Can schools of education provide quality CPD programming for diverse client groups? And, very importantly, (3) to what extent should schools of education be involved in CPD? These questions will be addressed from a deliberately limited perspective, that of our major schools of education. Our "leader" schools are those that have, over the years, gained prestige through their diverse doctoral programs and research and development activities. The position taken here is that the prospect for CPD in the sizable number of smaller and sometimes struggling institutions is closely linked to the fate of CPD in the major schools of education. If the potential for CPD exists at all, it will be found, at least initially, in the major schools of education. By virtue of their size and diverse expertise, they are more likely to have the necessary resources that might be realigned to address multiple, new objectives. Furthermore, by virtue of having key individuals in recognized leadership positions, these major schools may have the strength to rally the necessary institutional, political, and professional support for a new and broader mission.

WHY CONTINUING PROFESSIONAL DEVELOPMENT?

Schools of education have traditionally been defined by their commitment to the training of teachers, school administrators, and other specialists for work in elementary, secondary, and, to a lesser degree, postsecondary schools. Additionally, the major schools of education emphasize research and other services, such as dissemination of information and advocacy in special areas, to the education profession. These by no means constitute a narrow or unimportant mission. Yet there is definitely a press for a greatly expanded agenda, an agenda that would encompass service to several other professions and occupational areas. According to Dean Corrigan, a former president of the American Association of Colleges of Teacher Education and an active advocate:

> Leaders in schools, colleges, and departments of education (SCDEs) can no longer preside over their institutions in splendid isolation. Constructive relationships must

be established with the federal government, with private educational institutions, with public agencies in such fields as health, environment, welfare, housing, community planning, libraries, television, the performing arts, business, industry, and other settings which have up to now stood on the edges of the formal teaching, learning, and social services processes. . . . Elementary and secondary schools and colleges are now part of a system of continuing education for a large majority of America's people. SCDEs can become obsolete, or they can become the training and research arm of this new, expanding educational delivery system.[2]

In maintaining that there is a substantial body of educational knowledge and skill in schools of education that is generic and applicable to nonschool educational settings, Corrigan provides an example of what is called the *resource argument*. This argument rests on the contention that schools of education have considerable expertise in educational matters that is not fully utilized. In short, schools of education are obligated to articulate their resources better and to deliver their services more effectively.

The resource argument is closely related to what may be called the *substantive argument*, and both derive from the quest for generic skills. For example, teachers learn how to assess the needs of students in specific content areas and to plan appropriate instruction. Is this not a skill that could be used in educational projects in nonschool settings? Teachers learn how to motivate learners. Is this skill not extremely important in virtually all domains of working with adults? Teachers learn how to manage groups, organize time, keep records, develop materials, evaluate learner progress, speak with clarity, teach with enthusiasm, make formal presentations, conduct informal meetings, counsel students, and provide emotional support. These, of course, provide but a sampler of specific teacher skills that can be seen as relevant to optimal functioning in a broad range of occupations. Teachers learn these skills in schools of education; therefore, schools of education can provide training for personnel in many different types of occupations.

Furthermore, there are some who contend that the type of training provided by schools of education is not available anywhere else. This represents the *need argument*. It appears that most people serving educational purposes in nonschool settings have had little or no training specific to instruction. For example, trainers in industry have typically advanced into training positions based on their competence in a specific knowledge area. Training skills are usually picked up on the job. Some companies, often those with the most sophisticated training programs, view their trainers very seriously; serving successfully in a training function is one of the major steps on the ladder to upper management. At the same time, however, the number of corporate employees who view training as their primary career objective is typically quite small. It seems that training is perceived to be a management skill.

In nonschool settings, the education function is not clearly differentiated. There is probably merit in the position that business training programs, for example, would be stronger if training were identified as a specialty in its own right, if specific training for trainers were available, and if training were viewed as a prestigious career position. Enter the schools of education. There is a need, and schools of education have the resources for training trainers (generically, if you will) as well as teachers for elementary and secondary schools.

One of the most interesting and perhaps enticing rationales for schools of education to expand their CPD activities is the *big bucks argument*, which has been delineated by Robert Taylor and Rebecca Watts.[3] They quote from a market research report that industrial training is "one of the biggest businesses in the United States," and they estimate that close to $20 billion was spent in 1976 by industry and government to train 21 million employees. It would be nice if schools of education could tap this market, particularly since enrollments in traditional school of education programs have declined sharply in recent years.

All these arguments for CPD coalesce with the major problem all schools of education are fighting—their current lack of students. This general argument suggests that teacher training be more broadly conceived as providing interrelated human resource training or training for the helping professions. Therefore, schools of education should consider developing programs emphasizing the generic nature of teaching skills so that graduates will have a greater number of career options. Students could be trained not only as teachers but also as criminal justice workers, youth counselors, and industrial trainers, to name just a few. One wonders what weight the above arguments would carry if schools of education were not faced with the real prospect of retrenchment in the wake of declining enrollments in traditional programs.

CAN SCHOOLS OF EDUCATION PROVIDE QUALITY CPD?

One of the arguments presented in support of having schools of education explore the development of broader programs for CPD is that those schools have the resources. This contention needs to be thoroughly explored. Do schools of education—even major ones—really have the resources? Do they have the capacity to extend these resources into entirely new areas? Certain contextual issues must be addressed. Additionally, the experience of schools of education relative to CPD for educators working in school settings needs to be considered.

The Context

Any institution or institutional unit searching for new missions, attempting to clarify existing missions, or merely assessing the current state of the scene does so within a context. There are always institutional factors that argue for one type of decision or another: times are either prosperous or they are lean; students are either abundant or they are scarce; funds are either plentiful or they are dwindling; images are either powerful or they are being questioned. The list is endless. It suffices to note that contextual factors are important and should be considered by professors and administrators in schools of education as they chart future directions for continuing professional development in their institutions.

Schools of Education.   This is not a time of prosperity for schools of education. Enrollments are down, schools of education are attracting less able college students, and the image of education in general, and of teacher education in particular, appears considerably tarnished in the public eye.

The National Center for Education Statistics lists thirty-six intended areas of study for college-bound seniors. Rating college-bound seniors by Scholastic Aptitude Test (SAT) scores, those selecting professional education rank thirty-third.[4] The mean combined SAT scores for all college-bound seniors in 1981 was 890; for those selecting education, the figure was 809. Further, it is not only that students selecting education score lower than their collegiate colleagues, but also that the situation seems to be getting worse. The combined SAT scores for all students entering college between 1973 and 1981 declined approximately 3.9 percent. For those selecting education, the decline was 6.7 percent.

To anyone who teaches in a school of education, it is no secret that enrollments have been declining. In 1971, there were over 176,000 bachelor's degrees granted in education.[5] In 1980, just ten years later, that number had dropped to slightly over 118,000, a decline of over 33 percent. During that same period, bachelor's degrees in education as a percentage of all bachelor's degrees declined from 21 to 12.7 percent. Additionally, total university enrollments went from about 8.1 million to 10.5 million, an increase of approximately 29 percent. Thus, at a time when college and university enrollments were rising, bachelor's degree enrollments in education were dropping markedly. This situation certainly does not bode well for schools of education.

It is no secret that universities distribute funds unequally among programs. To the faculty member or administrator in a school of education, it is also no secret that schools of education are typically on the lower end of this unequal distribution. Although no one would claim that each university program should receive identical amounts of money, some do claim that schools of education get far too little of university resources. Bruce Peseau and Paul Orr ascribe numbers to this phenomenon that are quite dramatic. In 1977–78, the average cost of educating a teacher per academic year of instruction was $927. During that same year, approximately $1,400 was spent to educate the average American public school student.[6] Thus, teacher education students receive about one-third fewer dollars in support of their education than do typical third-grade students. The comparison is even more alarming when one compares the teacher education student to the equivalent full-time student in higher education. The teacher education student receives about 60 percent fewer dollars than does the typical university student. These data suggest that even in periods of declining enrollment, teacher education is still seen as a producer rather than a consumer of university revenue.

It should be obvious then that schools of education in many respects are not in a powerful position when it comes to making decisions about the future. They are getting fewer students, they are getting less able students, they are getting a very small share of the resources to teach students. And probably most importantly, the students they are enrolling today will be the teachers in need of continuing professional development tomorrow. Certainly, the picture is not rosy.

Relationship with the University. It probably comes as no surprise that schools of education are not typically viewed as being among the elite academic units in the university community. However, they have historically held a rather comfortable niche within the university because of their ability to produce revenues. Even though schools of education do not produce it at the level they once did, they still produce revenue.

In recent years, a few institutions have closed the doors to their schools or departments of education. Others are contemplating such a move. For those that survive, there is little to suggest that schools of education in major institutions can favorably alter their position on the resource allocation index relative to other units within the university. In fact, one can argue that the opposite is much more likely. One can be quite sure that university administrators will not allow the cost per student in schools of education to even approximate the per-student cost in other units in the university, for example, in engineering, architecture, management, or the arts and sciences. Could an administrator ever sell such a proposal to a university faculty senate, when the majority of the members—teachers themselves—are convinced that all one needs to do in order to teach is to master a content area thoroughly? Indeed, there are those in many academic units who believe that education courses are largely superfluous.

Thus, it would seem unrealistic to expect support for schools of education that seek program expansion or new missions. They also have problems within their own ranks and problems in dealing with the institutions that house and support them and that make important decisions about their future. Furthermore, an expanded CPD mission would most probably tread on the turf of other units of the university, for example, schools of social work and business. Clearly, the current status of schools of education and their historical place in the university community suggest that, if anything, the request will be to shrink further, to hunker down, to retrench.

Message from Context. Is there a message for leaders in schools of education that flows naturally from this analysis of context? Although it is becoming increasingly clear that significant and important changes will have to be made, these changes will have to be very carefully planned. Further, it appears that the catchwords for planning for the next decade will include cautiousness, prudence, and credibility. Schools of education will have to rethink and restate in very clear terms the nature of their mission. They will also have to develop programs consistent with their mission and, more importantly, demonstrate specifically the link between their activities and their mission. It is doubtful that there will be a great deal of support for new initiatives that transcend the traditional image of a school of education, particularly at this time when financial stress is being experienced in most units of the university. In fact, any attempt to begin new initiatives, to serve new clients, and to do things for which we are not prepared will most likely result in an institutional challenge to our credibility and our motivation. It would be a mistake to accept such a challenge, as our credibility is low enough already.

Continuing Development for School Professionals

Deans of major schools of education, in describing the activities of their faculties, frequently leave the impression that schools of education are cornucopias of CPD. It is true that various faculty members in schools of education frequently come in contact with practicing school teachers and administrators, especially those who enroll in degree programs and courses. But identifying the typical credit-bearing course as an example of "good" CPD (that is, timely and relevant to teaching in real schools) is probably stretching things a bit.

Graduate Courses and Degree Programs. Nearly all states have requirements for advanced courses beyond the initial teaching degree. A perusal of school of education catalogues could very well leave the impression that CPD for teachers and other professionals was being provided. There are, in fact, many courses available that could, in theory, upgrade the job performance of school professionals. However, in reality, school of education graduate courses and degree programs are not typically viewed as instruments for CPD. In many instances, courses are taken only by those who have a need to advance on a district salary scale. The courses selected are sometimes only remotely related to jobs in schools. Additionally, graduate degree programs are not typically viewed as a means to strengthen performance in the teaching role. Rather, they often serve as a means to move out of classroom teaching. In short, graduate courses, which in the abstract appear to provide a cornucopia of CPD for school personnel, have served other, usually overriding purposes. There is little to suggest that graduate courses have even begun to address the specific instructional needs of school professionals, as these needs emerge from actual work in schools.

Historically, CPD has not been well integrated with the substantive needs of practicing school professionals. To the extent that good CPD requires creativity and individuality in program planning, extensive knowledge about and involvement with the workaday world of the client, and collegial relationships with those in the field, it would seem that schools of education have not been terribly successful. Nearly anyone who is familiar with schools of education and their relationship to their constituents in the field realizes that provision of this type of CPD has been minimal at best. Their faculties typically have not been well "tuned in" to the needs of their clients relative to their current professional roles, and they have been perceived to be uninterested in what takes place in the field. Thus, graduate courses and programs, as mechanisms of CPD for school professionals, have in many ways contributed to the rather notable credibility gap that now separates schools of education from practicing school professionals.

Message from History.   Schools of education, through their graduate courses and programs, do have the structure for and a history of relating to practicing school professionals. In fact, however, very little has been done to develop programs that are geared to upgrading the skills of school personnel. Rather, the major impact of our graduate programs has been on role specialization outside the classroom and on teachers' career mobility. This is not to ignore the fact that some schools of education have developed exemplary in-service and staff development programs targeted specifically to meet the needs of schools and school personnel. However, these have been the exception rather than the rule. These special programs simply do not fit neatly into the institutional structure, and they usually do not last long.

Continuing Development for Nonschool Personnel

Considering the fiscal problems facing schools of education, the interest in serving new clients has become more intense. To many administrators, a move in this direction may appear to offer an "out," an escape from facing the painful alternative of retrenchment and faculty dismissals. As evidenced by name changes in some schools of education over recent years (for example, college of human services, college of education and allied professional studies), there has already been some movement in this direction. However, we believe that there are dangers inherent in expanding the mission of schools of education to serve the training needs of nonschool personnel. Our answer to the fundamental question of whether schools of education can provide quality CPD for nonschool personnel is—probably not.

An Analogy. Not so long ago, Chrysler Corporation was on the verge of bankruptcy. Would Chrysler have survived had it approached the problem through diversification into the production of other means of transportation, for example, trains, airplanes, and motorcycles? Assume it had been demonstrated that there was, in fact, a need for these products. Then, imagine a public relations campaign focused on (1) the fact that much of the technology and nuts and bolts supporting these various products are similar, that is, generic, (2) the argument that all that is really required is a multiple approach to assembling the basic components, and, finally, (3) the evidence that Chrysler has the resources and the will not only to produce these diverse products, but to produce them better than those companies already in these businesses. Of course, it would be hoped that the buying public would forget that Chrysler had not been particularly successful in marketing automobiles. We believe it naive to suggest that school of education faculties can easily and successfully gear up to address the CPD needs of nonschool personnel in any substantive manner at this time.

Track Record with School Professionals. For starters, schools of education have not served, in any meaningful way, the CPD needs of the education profession. While graduate-level courses and degree programs have made contributions to some practicing school professionals, for many others they have served primarily as the currency of exchange in salary and school career advancement. Whether the courses are good or bad, they are simply not typically regarded by anyone—professors, school administrators, teachers—as addressing the specific needs of schools. This is not to say that graduate-level courses are unimportant. We want our school personnel to be "educated" in the broadest, grandest sense of the term. However, standard graduate school courses are but one dimension of continuing professional development and are certainly not the most appropriate means of addressing the challenges and problems in American schools.

A recent, comprehensive study found that what school personnel need, want, and will participate in voluntarily are professional development activities that relate directly to current problems in specific schools and classrooms.[7] Teachers and administrators want professional development activities that have relevance and credibility and, not unimportantly, are available at times and in places that are convenient. These findings do not support semester-long general courses in, for example, reading methods, offered on a distant campus at 4 P.M., two days per week. Rather, there is a need for professional development activities, the content of which will be determined by specific need (for example, development of reading materials), for specific students (for example, primary grade, perceptually handicapped), and in a specific type of school (for example, Title I). Ideally, the program development activity should be offered at convenient sites (for example, schools) and at convenient times (for example, during the school day, perhaps with released time support).

Schools of education have not even begun to scratch the surface of program development appropriate to the CPD needs of the teaching profession. The expertise extant in faculties of schools of education has neither been described nor promoted, not to mention delivered, for the benefit of professional educators. Those who contend that schools of education are vast storehouses of expertise should take a close look at the underutilization of these resources by practicing education professionals. The track record is not good. It is naive to think that schools of education will be able to establish credible programming for nonschool personnel when they have not served well their natural and historical clients.

The Importance of Relevance. The generic skills argument offered in support of broad CPD efforts should also be challenged. Schools of education are already in trouble with their own constituency because of the widely held belief that many education courses are already too general. Offering courses for diverse client groups seemingly requires that these courses of necessity become even more nonspecific, that is, less related to any one participant's needs. Two program development axioms bear mention: to increase the number of potential enrollees, broaden the course (or program) objectives; to increase the value or impact of a course, narrow the course objectives. Obviously, these axioms are not compatible. In the case of CPD, good marketing and good program development do not always go hand in hand.

Nevertheless, the "generic wave" is now sweeping the country.

Although many of us, as consumers, will sometimes go generic as a cost-saving measure, do we not really prefer those products that are tailored to our particular needs and tastes? Generic products are not typically the products of choice. That we should even consider bringing generic programming to the training and CPD of teachers and other school personnel is suspect. Generic programming is likely to be disastrous not only for teacher training but also for all other occupational groups that happen to be pulled onto the bandwagon. We would end up not only with poorly trained teachers, but also with poorly trained mental health workers, criminal justice professionals, trainers in business, and any others who happened to be a product of these generic programs offered by schools of education.

The Necessity of Credibility.   There is yet another problem inherent in the generic skills argument as support for CPD across occupational groups. Incredibly, there seems to be some support for the hypothesis that professors in our schools of education can handle (albeit with a little "retooling") a vast multitude of content specialty areas. With a little cramming, our in-house specialist in behavior modification will easily be able to address the problems faced by criminal justice workers, or our group process expert will be able to address the needs of nursing supervisors. Even assuming these possibilities actually occur, can we imagine anyone finding these specialists credible?

There are certain dues to be paid in all lines of work, in all occupations and professions. These requirements may or may not be specified or, for that matter, even written down. However, those who have not had certain, specific experiences are simply not readily accepted by the culture. They do not have credibility. For instance, a professor with fifteen years' experience in developing specific instructional programs for schools and the military recently applied for a high-paying industrial training position. The application was dismissed—it was felt that the professor had no relevant experience. The most important criterion, it turns out, was work experience in a nonunion setting. The candidate with no training experience, but with experience as a supervisor of nonunion workers, got the job. The field of education is no different. What would be the chances of a successful chief executive officer of a large electronics firm when competing for a superintendency of schools? Better yet, look inside our own schools of education. How many faculty members would readily accept the claim of the professor of reading methods that he was also perfectly qualified to teach methods for secondary science? There is virtually no reason to expect that schools of education can serve the CPD needs of nonschool personnel, except in rare instances. It is not likely that even our major schools of education could rally the necessary institutional support for an expanded mission. Schools of education may have the need and the will to develop programs that will attract additional students. However, it is very questionable that they have the resources to serve such programs well.

SCHOOLS OF EDUCATION: REAFFIRMING THE TRAINING MISSION

The argument has been made that schools of education have neither the capacity nor the resources to support a mission expanded to include CPD for nonschool personnel. It is simply not feasible. Even more importantly, it would not be wise.

The Mission of Schools of Education

The mission of schools of education, as exemplified by our major universities, has evolved over the years. The university-based schools of education maintain a commitment to study the sociological, philosophical, historical, and psychological foundations of education. But also important to the mission is the training of teachers. Additionally, the research and development mission of these schools must not be underestimated. Given the importance of quality teaching and the sheer number of teachers in schools, one would also assume a major research agenda for teacher education. In fact, little has been accomplished, and a major challenge confronts our university-based schools of education in this regard. Over the years, the mission has expanded to include the training of school administrators and other education specialists. Recently, schools of education have become important in translating social change agendas into educational programs. The important question that must be asked is, "Do major university-based schools of education have a mission that includes CPD?"

Teachers, the primary products of our schools of education, are under intense public scrutiny. They endure perennial criticism. They need our support. A quest by schools of education for new client groups would almost certainly be viewed publicly as an attempt to "escape the sinking ship" of public education. It would not be unreasonable for professional organizations, policymakers, institutional administrators, and others to call into question the motives of schools of education for initiating a departure from service to their already troubled and beleaguered graduates and colleagues in the field. The argument has been made, although feebly, that schools of education would, in fact, not be deserting their primary client group. Rather, they would simply be adding new ones. The logic behind this position is difficult to untangle, particularly when one notes that, historically, schools of education have not been viewed as particularly effective in serving practicing school professionals. It would be difficult to explain how it is possible to undertake efforts in new directions, and at the same time serve more effectively those who have traditionally been our students.

As stated earlier, schools of education do not have strong credibility with practicing school professionals. If they were to publicize the initiative to serve other areas, this already tenuous relationship would become even more strained, and our lack of credibility would become more pronounced. Furthermore, there are absolutely no assurances— or even adequate reasons to believe—that new and strong support bases would be built in other occupational and service areas. Schools of education would then face the prospect of having virtually no support base within any profession. Is there anything to suggest that associations representing, for example, mental health workers or criminal justice professionals would come to view schools of education as their primary homes for professional training? This is very doubtful. At the same time, those organizations that traditionally and currently support practicing school professionals would very likely view a school of education expansion into other client areas as an abandonment of the commitment to the educational profession. They could be expected to work even less hard in the future than they have in the past to support high-quality professional training programs. In the long run it is most doubtful that schools of education could prosper under these circumstances.

Highlighting the Training Mission

Unlike other professional schools that provide training for practitioners (for example, medicine, law, engineering, architecture), schools of education exhibit no general congruence of opinion about curriculum, standards for promotion and tenure, and allocation of resources. Unfortunately too the commitment by schools of education to train practitioners is not as strong as it is in other professional schools housed within universities. The origin of schools of education in schools of arts and sciences is relevant here. Probably because of this heritage, we have adopted the liberal arts model of research and scholarly publication as the more valued professorial activities. Too often, we have conveniently overlooked or compromised the societal requisite, typically passed on through state legislatures and state boards of education, to prepare high-quality education professionals. Thus, while we have accepted training as a part of our mission, in actuality we tend not to value it highly nor to allocate resources to it in any meaningful way.

Yet it is difficult to conceive of either society or our collegial support base taking schools of education very seriously if we do not place considerable importance on the training mission. This is a particular problem in some of our prestigious schools of education where collegial discussion often centers on eliminating the professional training aspects of our mission. But it seems absolutely incongruous to foster the development of important research and scholarship while at the same time eschewing the mechanism (that is, training) that allows research and scholarship to be applied by school professionals. It is almost impossible to conceive of a school of education garnering prestige without offering quality training programs for school professionals. These would include, certainly, initial training programs, but also expanded programs for the continuing professional development of school personnel.

The relevant question, then, concerns whether we should alter, expand, or enhance our programs for CPD—not for noneducation clientele but for practicing school professionals. Should schools of education more fully accept as part of their mission the major problems confronting American schools? If the answer is yes, then markedly altered and expanded programs of CPD for school personnel appear to be a very legitimate part of that mission.

If schools of education do gear up to serve truly the CPD needs of school personnel, a major effort will be required. Our programs have not yet begun to serve the vast numbers of school personnel, who constitute, in fact, the largest occupational group in America. In America's elementary and secondary schools, there exists a need for high-quality CPD efforts. Their school personnel need the resources of schools of education. We cannot find a stronger, more needy audience anyplace else. The problem to be solved focuses on how schools of education can integrate the mission of enhanced CPD for school personnel with the equally important missions of initial training programs, research, scholarly pursuits, and legitimate service to the education profession and the university.

CONCLUSION

For purposes of integrity, as well as for the purpose of prosperity, it will be necessary for schools of education to retreat to a more focused stance on their historical mission, specifically, the training of education professionals at all levels, research and scholarly productivity relating to the field, and service to the education profession and to educational institutions. As we move ahead in the next decade, schools of education must not present the image of diluting their efforts by developing new missions conceived as "targets of opportunity." Rather, they must concentrate their efforts on the improvement of schooling.

America's schools of education cannot retreat from their primary reason for existence. Their willingness to restrict and focus their efforts will allow them to deal with the related problems of this crisis, such as leadership in the field, the maintenance of integrity, credibility with the public, and the improvement of elementary and secondary schools. It is difficult to imagine how expanding into CPD for other clients could do anything but magnify our problems to the point where they could potentially threaten the very existence of our schools of education.

NOTES

1. Dean C. Corrigan, "Preparing Educators for Nonschool Settings," in *Policy for the Education of Educators: Issues and Implications*, edited by Georgianna Appignani (Washington, D.C.: American Association of Colleges for Teacher Education, 1981), pp. 37-49.
2. Ibid., p. 47.

3. Robert E. Taylor and Rebecca L. Watts, "The Educational Needs of Business and Industry," in *Policy for the Education of Educators*, pp. 66-77.
4. Charles Hammer and Patricia L. Kuch, "Public Elementary/Secondary School Teachers," in *The Condition of Education, 1982 Edition*, edited by Nancy B. Dearman and Valena White Plisko (Washington, D.C.: National Center for Education Statistics, 1982), pp. 85-115.
5. Edith M. Huddleston, "Postsecondary Education," in *Condition of Education*, pp. 117-165.
6. Bruce Peseau and Paul Orr, "The Outrageous Underfunding of Teacher Education," *Phi Delta Kappan* 62 (October 1980):100-102.
7. Sally K. Mertens and Sam J. Yarger, *Teacher Centers in Action* (Syracuse, N.Y.: Syracuse Area Teacher Center, Syracuse University, 1981).

PART II

Human Services and Colleges of Education

INTRODUCTION

Under major consideration in some colleges of education is the relationship between education and other human service professions and the contributions that can be made by educators to the preparation of those professionals as well as to the preparation of educators who will be employed in human service organizations other than schools. In some universities there have been systematic responses to this issue; in others it appears that such efforts have been little more than relabeling existing courses in the hopes of attracting more students. Some faculty members in colleges of education believe that this expansion of mission will detract from the primary mission of serving the nation's schools and that education faculty members are not prepared to render appropriate service to other human service professions.

The many efforts to move from curative to preventive care indicate a major shift in the human service professions. This shift inevitably highlights an educational function that is important both to professionals in most human service areas and to their clients. The expansion of a preventive approach in most human service professions, as well as the focus on human resource development in many profit and nonprofit organizations, and the educational expertise inherent in these functions present not only opportunities for colleges of education but quite possibly a responsibility as well.

Lawrence Cremin in his *Public Education* (1976) stressed the necessity to redefine public education in broader terms to reflect more accurately the current reality where learning and teaching are lifelong activities that occur in most of society's institutions. As society continues to change and develop, so do its service structures. It seems that the present is an appropriate time to reconceptualize education, the roles of educators, and the preparation of educators within this broader context.

The four chapters in Part II offer an opportunity to think about developments in four human service areas: health care, mental health, youth services, and training and development. The authors were asked to describe the trends and opportunities in their respective areas. As educators, we can examine these descriptions to see what educational needs are inherent in them and to explore ways in which professional educators can assist in meeting those needs. This exploration can serve as a starting point for interprofessional dialogue, planning, and action. We ask the reader to view these chapters in this way.

Tom Weirath and Owen Levin argue in Chapter 6 that the health care system has been changing so rapidly that there is a great need to rethink the educational preparation and continuing education of providers as well as of consumers of health care. As they note: "The state of complete physical and mental well-being [is] not merely the absence of disease or infirmity." This change has required changes in definition, thinking, structure, participants, tasks, and functions. They describe five areas where the knowledge and skills of educators are increasingly necessary: the reorientation of life-style, the health education function in health maintenance organizations, continuing education for health providers, health education for the public, and education for effective public participation on regulatory and policy-making boards. They assert that, while providers of health care are not educators and educators are not health care providers, both should understand their mutual roles.

Darold Treffert provides a history and review of the trends in beliefs about mental health and about the treatment of mental illness. He traces the progression from categorical disability systems to human service orientations and programs. The parallel progression among professionals has been increasingly from those who provide generalist services to those who offer highly specialized services. There is now a realization that the mental health system needs both generalists and specialists, with the generalist being the first point of contact for the client. This progression is similar to that taking place in medicine—from the general practitioner to specialists to a combination of family practitioners and specialists who provide a balanced partnership. Treffert notes that the "holistic" practitioner or generalist is part health educator and part health practitioner—a concept that is supportive of one of the roles for colleges of education as proposed in the final chapter of this volume. Treffert describes what he calls a "sane asylum," which is premised on prevention rather than on cure. In his implementation of such an institution in Wisconsin, Treffert involved a number of professionals who had backgrounds in education and counseling.

Robert Carlson documents the fragmentation and insufficiency of youth services. He describes the unclear definitions of youth utilized by various institutions, as well as the confused attitudes toward youth. He believes that the same lack of focus pervades the research on the needs and problems of youth. In youth services the attention to prevention is far less than is currently the case in most human service areas. Carlson contends that historical divisions among professionals who serve youth act as a barrier to understanding youth in a more holistic fashion. He suggests that youth should serve as a unifying theme through which multiple institutions and professional identities could be utilized in an integrated way. He provides some generic competencies to guide such exploration.

Leonard Nadler examines the history of training and human resource development in business, industry, labor unions, government, and voluntary organizations. He makes distinctions among the functions of training, education, and development and indicates the roles and competencies required if those functions are to be adequately performed in the area of human resource development. He portrays the field of human resource development as one that is expanding rapidly in its emphases yet is still in a stage of confusion. That confusion, however, offers colleges of education an opportunity to provide more deliberate and systematic preparation of personnel for work in human resource development.

Trends in Health
Delivery Systems

Tom Weirath and Owen Levin

BACKGROUND

Before World War I, health care was relatively simple in terms of treatment and the occupations available to deliver it. Medical specialties were nonexistent, as were most of the allied health professions. Nursing was essentially a palliative occupation. Hospitals were not the focus of health care delivery, nor were they places where the recovery and rehabilitation of patients were expected. Rather, they were institutions for the terminally ill and the dying poor.

The Flexner Report in 1910, however, changed medical education and was one catalyst that helped shape contemporary medical education. It placed emphasis on the scientific approach to medical education and advocated standards for medical schools in terms of the essential curriculum. The biological and natural sciences were considered the critical foundation for the physician.[1]

Thirty years ago, the health care system consisted of physicians, nurses, chiropractors, and optometrists. The health care system and the practitioners of today, however, bear little resemblance to their historical counterparts. Advances in technology have fostered the

specialization of physicians and nurses and contributed to the creation of allied health occupations and specialties unheard of, even
inconceivable, thirty years ago. Currently, there are approximately 5
million health care workers in this country in 222 different occupations.[2] Included in these are occupations as diverse as physicians,
physician's assistants, health educators, and medical illustrators.
Virtually all health occupation categories are experiencing some
growth and are providing a variety of career opportunities. The
number of physicians, for example, increased 67 percent between
1950 and 1973, a period during which the population increased only
37 percent.[3] It is projected that the number of physicians will grow
nearly 84 percent between 1975 and 1990.[4] This projection—not just
speculation—includes those physicians who are already in the lengthy
training process and who will be practicing medicine in 1990.

This increase in physicians has been interpreted to mean that
persons for whom medical care has previously not been available will
now be able to receive it. Unfortunately, this has not happened, at
least in many rural and inner-city areas, even though the overall ratio
of physicians to population has improved. What has become clear is
that the cost and geographical distribution of physicians are not
controlled by traditional economic market forces.

As a result of this realization, attention has become increasingly
directed to the high cost of health care. No longer is there public or
governmental willingness to accept the assumption that the goal of a
healthy population is achieved through a "blank check" approach.
For the period 1950–77, health care costs increased from approximately 4.5 to 9.3 percent of the gross national product.[5] Recent data
have it approaching 10 percent. Concern about health care costs has,
ironically, contributed to an expansion of the health system. The
development of strategies to reduce or at least stabilize costs has
generated a demand for health economists, health planners, hospital
administrators, and other professions. The perceived high cost of
health care is leading to the development and widespread use of
alternatives such as health maintenance organizations (HMOs) and
the increased use of physician's assistants, nurse midwives, and nurse
practitioners to deliver medical care. There is evidence, however, that
the glut of physicians in some areas is now causing displacement of
(and reduced opportunities for) these mid-level health practitioners.
Because of third-party reimbursement practices, too, physicians have

a competitive edge and can carve out a large market share of providing health services.

How can this phenomenon occur? The answer lies with medical practice and the public's perception of the health care system. As medicine became more scientific and specialized, its early successes increased manifold. The public was optimistic, fed by successes in the control of communicable disease and advances in technology for the diagnosis and treatment of illness. The result was the deification of the physician and the medicalization of health and the health care system. In a sense, health care became a matter for professionals; the public felt less of a responsibility for their health, confident that some professional (under a physician's direction) would cure them if they became ill. Traditional medicine thus developed as an *ex post facto* system, a system that is reactive, not active. Medical intervention occurs when patients present their symptoms to a physician. The symptoms presumably have a physiological or biological origin.

More recently, health has been defined by the World Health Organization (WHO) as something more than the absence of a diseased condition. The definition of health now generally subscribed to is: "the state of complete physical and mental well-being and not merely the absence of disease or infirmity."[6] This country still depends on a definition that considers access to care; but if the implications of the WHO definition are considered, the magnitude of health care is broadened beyond the traditional disease-centered approach for which the physician is centrally responsible. Specifically, the WHO orientation to health expands the boundaries of the elements and occupations to be included under the rubric of the health care system. Occupations as diverse as physicians, hospital administrators, health educators, environmental engineers, and health economists are included under this definition of health care. Likewise, institutions as diverse as hospitals, medical schools, and health planning agencies have to be considered in order to gain a full understanding of the dynamics of the health care system.

The shifting view of health is not the only factor in the changing structure of the health care system. The escalating costs of health care also have an impact. The high costs of health care serve as an impetus for rethinking what services are delivered, who delivers them, and through what structures and in what manner health care is delivered. Likewise, the changing definition of health has led to a rethinking of which tasks and functions are required to assure a quality health care system and, as a consequence, a healthy population. It is no longer acceptable to equate health with the sum total of health care services provided. Experience has shown a lack of a demonstrable relationship between the process of delivering health services and a resultant outcome of health. Even more important, though subtle, "quality care" is being minimized in favor of terms like "adequacy" and "efficiency" as government strives to effect cost-containment.

EDUCATIONAL IMPLICATIONS OF HEALTH SYSTEM TRENDS

Health professionals, regulators, and consumers need knowledge and information to deal effectively with and function within the existing and emerging health care system. This is illustrated graphically when one considers that the output of the health care system is the product of tasks and interactions of some 222 types of health professionals. The general kinds of information that must be available to the actors within this system include: first, the *communication of norms* to all practitioners, teachers, and institutions in the health care field, and to all consumers of the health care system; second, information to facilitate *changes in behavior, knowledge, and skills*; and, last, the *coordination* of communication and changes between and among professionals, programs, third-party payors, regulators, and consumers.

The health care system has changed and is continuing to change so rapidly that professionals and consumers within the health care system are in constant need of education and educational preparation. Education is or will increasingly become necessary in at least five different areas:

1. Health life-style reorientation for government and the general public

2. Health education in health maintenance organizations and alternative delivery settings

3. Continuing education for providers

4. Public education

5. Educating citizens and providers for participation in regulatory and policy boards

The following sections will examine each of these areas in terms of the kind of education needed and the implications for the numbers and types of additional health personnel.

Health Life-style Reorientation

Modern medicine has made dramatic advances during the last few decades. This success is reflected in the advances of medical technology, for example, Computerized Axial Tomography (CAT) scanners, surgical techniques, transplantation of organs, and the conquering of infectious diseases. Through medical research, great strides have been made in determining the cause and prevention of disease, such as the development of the polio vaccine. Though modern medicine has made significant advances in identifying the causes of many illnesses, nevertheless, there remain many illnesses whose causes are difficult to discover and whose cures remain only remote possibilities. The current health care system is often characterized as being highly specialized, fragmented, and costly. Moreover, its high cost has not been associated with a commensurate improvement in the population's health status.

The failure of the traditional, reactive medical care system to maintain a healthy population forces a rethinking of health care strategies for assuring a healthy population. One alternative to the orientation of the medical model of health care is reflected in the WHO definition of health. This definition emphasizes a more preventive approach to health care in the hope of reducing the number of persons who are treated in the expensive, reactive *ex post facto* medical care system.

A concern for both the well-being of the population and the containment of cost is forcing the health care system to place more emphasis on primary and secondary prevention. Primary prevention focuses on environmental, immunological, nutritional, and life-style strategies for preventing the development of conditions conducive to illness or disease. It also refers to efforts to improve and enhance the quality of life. Environmental, immunological, and nutritional strategies are traditionally associated with primary prevention more than is the relatively recent focus on life-style orientation. If a reorientation of life-style has the potential to improve overall health status and reduce costs, then information on its value and the means to achieve it must be identified and communicated to health providers, consumers, and educators themselves. Of course, budget pressures make it difficult to maximize preventive efforts, but there still remains strong interest.

Secondary prevention involves the treatment of those who have high-risk potentials to develop particular diseases, such as diabetes and high blood pressure. Efforts are made to treat such persons at the earliest possible time, rather than wait for symptoms to appear or for curative medical intervention to be needed.

The new orientation to preventive health care represents a clear departure from traditional health care. Change in perception, attitudes, and practices of providers, consumers, and educators is necessary. Providers and consumers must recognize the limits of the traditional medical care system and accept the fact that medicine, by itself, cannot solve many health problems. Specifically, providers as well as consumers must recognize that consumers have a responsibility for their own health condition. There are individual actions that the consumer can take to prevent illness or at least reduce the likelihood of disease. The traditional medical orientation fosters a dependency by the consumer on physicians, hospitals, and ancillary personnel. Consumers abuse or neglect their bodies, become ill or diseased, and then expect physicians and medical technology to repair and restore them to a predisease state.

Health care providers and consumers must be exposed to sound information about how *environmental* and *sociocultural* factors can and do affect a population's health.[7] If this information is successfully communicated, then *intervention strategies* for *changing life-styles* can be communicated to both providers and consumers. This is not an easy task. The relationships between environmental and sociocultural factors and health are often unclear. Relationships may appear to be indirect or based on tenuous arguments. An appropriate response or action may be unknown or unattractive. Using drugs and other medical technology to intervene in disease conditions is more concrete and has more immediate effects. The effects of life-style reorientation, if any at all, are long term. Ideally, cost containment will force less expensive means of corrections.

Before providers and consumers can be informed, educators must be informed. Physicians and nurses increasingly recognize the need for health education and preventive care. But, in reality, there is a two-part question: who provides health education, and who *should* provide it. Most physicians have neither the time nor the training to be effective health educators. Professional nurses, especially those with postbaccalaureate training, usually have some training in health education. Unfortunately, these professionals are not widely available or effectively used, often as a result of archaic licensing practices or inadequate reimbursement by third-party payors. In addition, there are large numbers of social workers, psychologists, counselors, and health educators who are becoming part of a larger and increasingly fragmented health care system. Further complicating matters is the fact that patient care reimbursement mechanisms do not generally encourage such nonmedical intervention.

The providers of health care are not trained educators, and trained educators are not health professionals. The initial step, therefore, will be for both educators and the providers to understand the roles each may play in the health care system and to appreciate the contribution each makes or could make to achieve and maintain the health of the population.

Health Education in the HMO Setting

Health maintenance organizations (HMOs) accept contractual responsibility for the health of an enrolled population in exchange for a fixed, prepaid sum of money, assuring the delivery of a full range of health care services.[8]

Over the past decade, there has been a growing recognition of the HMO concept as a way of improving the efficiency of the present health care delivery system. These organizations, which are now providing health services to more than 6.4 million people, currently operate under a variety of organizational and financial mechanisms and have been developed with public and private funds. Research has shown that HMOs can provide a significant alternative in a restructured and more cost-effective health care delivery system because they help reduce the rate of utilization of expensive health services, such as hospital care, and they provide a more balanced mixture of ambulatory and other health care services. The HMO also can more effectively use nonphysician practitioners and apply health education principles. In a HMO, enrollees must be educated to use preventive services and to seek care in the early stages of illness. Enrollees need to be encouraged to change life-styles and behaviors that do not promote a high level of wellness. It is in the HMO setting that the reorientation to wellness holds the greatest promise.

The stake of the federal government in promotion of the HMO

setting is high. Each HMO seeking federal qualification must employ a health educator and have a plan for health education. Without such a plan, the HMO is merely a reimbursement mechanism. Health educators in HMOs have tended to be nurses, but, as HMOs expand, one may expect the need for persons trained in educational theory to grow.

Members of HMOs must be educated to use preventive services, but consumers outside the HMO setting must also be informed about the viability of the HMO as an alternative to the present health care delivery system. If a HMO is a cost-effective way to deliver quality health care, then its advantages must be highlighted and its myths of impersonality and inadequate care must be debunked. The role of the HMO in the larger health care system must be appreciated. As a type of health care delivery system, the HMO contrasts sharply with the traditional model of the private practice of a physician. A HMO should not be an impersonal system with little concern for the consumer-subscriber, as it is often portrayed or perceived. Erroneous perceptions must be refuted and the value of alternative delivery systems communicated to both providers and consumers. Negative impressions may fade as participation in HMOs by Medicaid users, public employees, and workers in private industry grows.

The role of the HMO requires that it communicate with and educate diverse publics. To many providers and consumers of health care, the HMO is a foreign idea, an idea for which there is no frame of reference. This new idea and alternative must be taught. Many opportunities exist, therefore, in changing practices and in embracing needed changes in the system. In many instances, however, consumers are being pushed or even locked into HMO plans or prepaid arrangements. It is too early to determine if expectations are being met. It is also true that if everyone were enrolled in a HMO, there would be no private fee-for-service as a basis of comparison, and the effectiveness of the HMO could decline. Policymakers of the future will have to deal with ways of keeping the competition to HMOs alive.

Continuing Education for Providers

In addition to the problems of spiraling costs, a concern also exists about assuring the quality of health care and maintaining and improving the competence of all practicing health workers. As physicians and other professionals are increasingly called upon to guide their clients through the health care system, their ability to do so is determined by their knowledge and understanding of the system. Health care practice and technology are rapidly changing. With over 5 million health care workers in this country in 222 occupational classifications, the problems of reaching health workers with information necessary to update knowledge is enormous. This process presumes that appropriate information is available, that it is in an appropriate form, and that there are adequate mechanisms and trained personnel to deliver it. It must also be remembered that information is not synonymous with changed behavior—the necessary outcome of education. The knowledge and expertise of professional educators is needed.

One mechanism commonly used to guarantee some minimal level of competence for occupations is state licensure. However, experience with licensing has proved that it has limited value in the maintenance of competence or the assurance of quality care. Some occupations are regulated while others are not. In many regulated occupations, interpretations of licensing practice acts have limited occupational entry, geographic mobility, and any appropriate delegation of responsibility. Such licensing regulation has certainly contributed to increased health care costs. After years of piecemeal efforts, only a fragmented, uncoordinated system of occupational licensing exists. A study done in Wisconsin by a special legislative committee on occupational licensing in 1977 adopted tenets that occupations should be regulated by the state only when:

1. Their unregulated practice can clearly harm or endanger the health, safety, and welfare of the public and when the potential for such harm is easily recognizable and not remote or dependent upon tenuous argument.

2. The public needs, and will benefit by, an assurance of initial and continuing professional and occupational ability.

3. The public cannot be effectively protected by other means.

4. It can be demonstrated that occupational licensing would be the most appropriate form of regulation.[9]

It is apparent that many requirements used by existing licensing boards are not necessarily job-related, nor are they always valid and reliable. State licensure alone is insufficient. Consequently, other mechanisms that may assure occupational competence must be explored.

One option has been to require continuing education courses. As a result, continuing education programs have proliferated at many universities and colleges. These programs can be viewed as a partnership between educators in institutions and practitioners in the field, a partnership necessary to determine the type of health education offered, as well as when, where, and under what circumstances. The area of continuing education could be characterized as a growth industry, and opportunities for instructors may be available in this area. However, the sufficiency of the continuing education strategy as an effective way to maintain competence is increasingly being questioned. No compelling evidence has been presented that shows continuing education has a positive effect on either the way providers practice or the outcomes of their efforts.[10]

Evaluation of continuing education courses should be a high priority. Persons trained in evaluation methodologies and the development of effective, necessary continuing education courses are required. In addition, persons who are educated in job testing and job analysis will become necessary to aid state licensing boards to improve their effectiveness. Educators can be used to test and validate instruments used by licensing and regulatory boards in the evaluation of the competence of health professionals. In addition, educators may be consulted to analyze the effectiveness of administrative rules and provider-practice acts. Consumers are at a distinct disadvantage in this arena, especially when providers take offense under the guise of having expert knowledge. Organizations like Professional Review Organizations may also require the skills of educators to analyze data collected, interpret data, and communicate their significance to health providers, planners, and consumers. Health planning and utilization review requirements under federal law are in a state of flux and will change in the next few years, but the need for both—and professionals to work in these areas—will remain, regardless of state or federal law.

Public Education

A fourth area of need is public education about appropriate access to and use of the health care system. The importance of this educational process has been alluded to in previous sections. The task before the educator is no easy one. The health care system is in many ways a nonsystem. To attempt to identify its boundaries is an almost impossible task. Whatever system that may have once existed has developed, over the last quarter century, into a fragmented and uncoordinated conglomeration of providers and settings. All of these confront uninformed consumers with an array of choices requiring decisions that they may be uncomfortable in making. Minorities, the poor, and the aged are particular target populations for a new educational emphasis. Schools, public and voluntary health agencies, mental health associations, social service agencies, and unions are the types of organizations that may be used to channel information about the health care system to segments of the public.

Information about the health care system that may be required by the public is diverse. The most obvious application for education would enable persons to cope with illnesses, especially chronic diseases. Education should emphasize the available strategies for coping with chronic illness, specifically self-care strategies designed to keep the patient out of the more expensive components of the health care system, such as hospitals.

Education involves much more than simply providing information, which all too often becomes simply a substitute for education. Understanding and retaining sufficient information on which to base an informed choice, and then acting accordingly, are difficult, but it is the aim of true education.

A more general type of education is needed for the public at large. Our medical care system has, until recently, emphasized the dependency of the client in the patient-provider relationship. As noted previously, the view has been one of the health consumer becoming ill, diseased, or injured, with the expectation that the medical care system will provide repair and rehabilitation. Responsibility for one's own health condition is not commonly accepted. Before educating the general public as to available preventive and health care strategies, however, it may be necessary to convince individuals that they do have responsibility for their own physical, mental, and social condition.

To develop a level of public education that achieves the proper balance between self-care and dependency is a most serious challenge to health professionals and educators. Identifying those situations for which self-care is appropriate and sufficient and those for which dependence upon providers is appropriate and sufficient should be a continuing challenge and struggle.

Educating Health Consumers for Political Participation

One other area appropriate for health education is that of the politics of health care. Most consumers tend to believe that the essence of the health care system is the provision of services from physicians to patients. However, the expanding definition of health care, the increasing number of services interpreted as health care services, the increasing numbers and types of health professions, and the expanding role of federal and state government all require that the political and organizational aspects of the health care system be clearly understood. Only by understanding the political and organizational aspects of this system does the consumer have an opportunity to find a way through its maze and to participate meaningfully in decisions. Knowing why the system is effective or ineffective requires knowledge about its social and political contexts. In turn, understanding the social and political contexts in which health care is delivered may provide some insight into the high or low quality of services.

Because of the expanded role of the state and federal government in the regulation of the health care system and to foster the developing interest of the health care consumer in the operation of this system, knowledge about the political dynamics of health care must be transmitted to the public. Consumers—and entire regulatory boards such as Health Systems Agencies and State Health Coordinating Councils—need to be aware of their purpose and role in the regulation of the health industry. Even though laws and requirements are changing, and the actual shape of health planning and advisory bodies may change, the need for education remains. Government is always trying to identify and educate consumers to articulate public needs and concerns in an arena largely dominated by the health care provider.

Specifically, consumers need to be sensitized to the impact of their decisions on the supply of health personnel, on the demand for provider services, and on the real cost to society. Sophisticated providers have their professional associations and organizations—as well as peer support—to bolster their positions. Consumers need equally strong and readily available support in order to make the regulatory and planning system work. Creating such support is an extremely large task.

Another level of citizen participation involves consumer advocacy—whether for the needs of specific minority populations or for those of the general population. Ombudsman programs, established with public or private support, can explain to various populations how to use the health care system, what their rights and obligations are, and how to articulate their needs before health care institutions and policy-making bodies.

A final area for citizen participation is the legislative political arena. Elected representatives make decisions every day that affect health and the health care system. Often, decisions are based on information provided by lobbyists, pressure groups, and, more episodically or inconsistently, professional health planners. Health care education should be appropriately focused at elected representatives at all levels of government.

The task of educating the consumer about the political and organizational aspects of the health care system is a large one. But the nature of this need for information is far removed from what is commonly thought to be the essence of health care—the physician-patient relationship. As a consequence, the consumer may have little appreciation of how political and organizational aspects may affect the kind of health care received. The task of the health educator will be to persuade the consumer of the relevance of this type of knowledge. Once this is done, the consumer must be shown how information may be used to influence the nature of the health care system. Without an appreciation of political and organizational dynamics, health consumers are guaranteed a high level of frustration when they attempt to influence the outcome of the decision-making process. Therefore, information about the way health care organizations operate and about effective political strategies and tactics for influencing the decision making is a practical necessity.

SUMMARY

It should be clear that the health care system has reached a point where it can no longer afford to ignore educational theory—even though the system may have backed into this realization for reasons such as cost containment. It is equally clear that traditionally trained health professionals are inadequately prepared to educate clients and their professional peers. The health care system is undergoing significant changes in areas of government regulation and reimbursement, delivery of care, professional education, public education, and citizen involvement in decision making. These changes demand restructuring the system to provide incentives for a new emphasis on costcontainment and accountability. The outcomes of these changes include a greatly expanded demand for health educators and health professionals trained in educational principles and practices.

Markets for such personnel will be found in medical and dental practices, in local school systems, in home care agencies, in industrial health (occupational safety and health promotion) settings, in acutecare and specialty-care institutions, in family planning agencies, in drug and poison information centers, in planning and regulatory agencies, in educational institutions, and in almost any other institution or organization that delivers human services.

Health education needs are growing and are limited only to the extent to which educators aggressively and creatively pursue ways of influencing the health care system. Health professionals are all attempting to "deliver" health education, which may often limit a health educator's ability to do "hands on" educating. But there are myriad opportunities to teach health professionals and to deal directly with other educational needs. Health educators do not necessarily represent a discipline, but a plethora of needs in search of persons willing to address them.

NOTES

1. Ken White, "Health Care Arrangements in the United States: A.D. 1972," in "Medical Care and Medical Cure," *Milbank Memorial Fund Quarterly* 50 (October 1974):19. See also, Abraham Flexner, *Medical Education in the United States and Canada* (New York: Carnegie Foundation for the Advancement of Teaching, 1910).
2. *Trends Affecting the U.S. Health Care System* (Rockville, Md.: Health Resources Administration, U.S. Department of Health, Education, and Welfare, 1976).
3. Ibid., p. 342.
4. Martha Katz, David C. Warner, and Dale Whittington, "The Supply of Physicians and Physicians' Incomes," *Journal of Health Politics, Policy, and Law* 2 (Summer 1977):227–56.
5. Zachary Dyckman, *Physicians: A Study of Physician Fees* (Washington, D.C.: Council on Wage and Price Stability, 1978), p. i.

6. Rick Carlson, *The End of Medicine* (New York: Wiley, 1975), p. 181.

7. For an example of the importance of understanding these factors for health, see Frederick Sargent III, "Man–Environment Problems for Public Health," *American Journal of Public Health* 62(5) (1972):626–33.

8. See, for example, Paul Feldstein, *Prepaid Group Practice: An Analysis and Review* (Ann Arbor, Mich.: University Bureau of Hospital Administration, 1971).

9. Wisconsin Legislative Council, *Legislation Relating to Occupational Licensing* (Madison, 1977).

10. National Symposium on Relicensure and the Continuing Education of Health Service Professionals, University of California, San Francisco, December 2–3, 1978.

CHAPTER 7

Trends in Mental Health Systems

Darold A. Treffert

BACKGROUND

Perhaps the best way to understand where the field of mental health is headed and what opportunities, implications, and possibilities the future may hold for professional educators is to look at where it has been.

There have been four major revolutions in the care of the mentally ill. The first occurred in the eighteenth century in the work best exemplified by a French psychiatrist, Philippe Pinel, who is often characterized in pictures and posters as freeing the mentally ill from their chains when he was superintendent of the *Bicêtre* (for male patients) and later of the *Salpêtrière* (for females), institutions that housed together criminals, mentally retarded patients, and the mentally ill. Pinel and others began to separate the "mad" from the "bad," building special facilities (asylums) for the care and treatment of the mentally ill. The asylum, "a place of security and retreat" (a warm term, really), began to appear first in Europe. The first such facility in the American colonies exclusively for mental patients was opened in Williamsburg, Virginia, in 1773. Following that, each state established one or more Insane Asylums or Lunatic Asylums, as they generally were called. Each resembled another because they shared the same architectural features, the so-called Kirkbride architecture, named after Dr. Thomas Kirkbride who designed the first such building in West Philadelphia in 1841.

Contrary to popular belief, the early asylum was not the cold, foreboding, and hopeless place so often associated with that term, but rather a place of security and retreat for persons who were ill, disabled, or unable to make it in what even then was a competitive society. The original planners of the hospital that I once administered, for example, spoke merely of choosing a pastoral, lakeshore site away "from the hustle and bustle and commotion of things, near blooming and growing things. A place to restore the spirit for people broken on the wheels of living." Planners of this hospital generously allotted an acre of land per patient; the rather stingy, present-day standard is 100 square feet per patient room. Because asylums, at least in this country, were never sufficiently funded, getting away got turned into being put way, and the term *asylum*, even the concept, became disreputable. Since the treatment of mental illness was almost nonexistent, the asylum became a place to house, not keep, the mentally ill. An era of descriptive psychiatry prevailed; elaborate descriptions were made of mental illness, but very little was available therapeutically to treat the illness itself. The asylum—underfunded, isolated, and probably hopeless—became a place where mental illness was elaborately described, but not treated.

That scene set the stage for the second revolution in psychiatry. Sigmund Freud, a neurologist who became interested in causes of certain kinds of hysterical paralysis, began to inquire about the process of insanity, its causes, and its treatment. Rather than merely describing illness and measuring skull size or looking for Darwinian tubercles (in vogue in the early 1900s), Freud brought inquiry and treatment to some kinds of mental illness, principally the neuroses, and spawned a mass effort to understand, rather than merely describe, the mentally ill. Emphasis shifted away from the soma to the psyche, and a whole body of psychoanalytic theory and practice emerged. Practitioners, and to some extent the public, became more interested, even intrigued with mental illness, and a more hopeful, positive, and inquisitive atmosphere began to prevail. Whether Freud's theories were correct or incorrect, they captured the imagination of enough persons so that psychiatry began to gain popularity as a science and specialty. As a consequence, mental illness ceased to be viewed as a degenerative, invisible disease.

The third revolution in psychiatry occurred in 1955 with the introduction of the so-called "tranquilizers." The first major tranquilizer, chlorpromazine (Thorazine), was discovered in the process of finding a better antihistamine, one with a less sedating effect. In tests of chlorpromazine in the laboratory, animals became "tranquil" rather than sedated, creating the new possibility that medications might specifically treat anxiety in humans. Thorazine and the myriad of drugs that have followed were introduced to treat schizophrenia, the most pervasive and crippling of the mental disorders; soon thereafter, antidepressant drugs were introduced to treat another prevalent major mental illness, depression.

Largely as a result of the discovery of antipsychotic and antidepressant medications, state and county mental hospital populations, which had peaked at a population of 557,000 patients in 1955, began to diminish for the first time in a 175-year period. These populations decreased despite an increased admission rate. This dramatic downward trend—from nearly 600,000 patients to less than half that number by 1973, and to less than one-third that number by 1978—was a direct result of the introduction of the antipsychotic and antidepressant medications. While they cured neither schizophrenia nor depression, these drugs did make it possible to treat and control symptoms. The typical length of a patient's hospitalization began to be measured in terms of days or weeks rather than months or years. As the treatment of mental illness became more hopeful, the hospitals where that treatment was practiced became more hopeful places. Greater numbers of practitioners were attracted to the field of mental health. Psychiatrists in the United States, as one illustration of a group of practitioners, grew in number from only a few such specialists in the 1870s to more than 25,000 in 1978. The general attitude of communities toward the mentally ill also became much more hopeful. Persons released from specialized mental health facilities to their communities could be treated with antipsychotic and antidepressant medications, typically in community aftercare clinics, and general hospitals began to admit directly and care for psychiatric patients.

The third revolution made possible the fourth revolution, that of community psychiatry. Community psychiatry is based on a set of principles relating to patient care. The patient should be treated as close to his or her own home as possible, in the least restrictive environment possible, in the shortest duration of time possible, and with the least possible disruption to his or her life. Emphasis on prolonged in-patient care with only brief or nonexistent aftercare has been replaced by an emphasis on brief in-patient care with prolonged aftercare. Stimulated and supported by mental health center funding created and promoted by President John F. Kennedy through the National Institute of Mental Health, a whole new system of eventually 1,500 community mental health centers grew throughout the country and became an increasingly important part of the spectrum of mental health services available to the mentally ill. The work place of the practitioner became the clinic and the community, not just the hospital.

New approaches, new systems, and new disciplines began to emerge. The community mental health center, with a growing emphasis on treatment, began to focus on education and prevention, as well as treatment. A team concept developed wherein the psychiatrist did not work as an independent practitioner, but rather used, whenever and wherever possible, the skills of other team members, such as psychologists, social workers, psychiatric nurses, occupational therapists, recreational therapists, music therapists, rehabilitation specialists, and a full variety of other disciplines. This has allowed a more comprehensive and holistic approach to the care of the mentally ill patient.

These trends, systems, and disciplines cast the future for mental health programming. The professional educator should not only be cognizant of them but also help create, shape, and mold them. What is a trend today will be the manner of practice tomorrow.

NEWER TRENDS, SYSTEMS, AND DISCIPLINES

From Categorical Disability Systems to Human Service Systems

Probably the most prevalent present trend is for mental health treatment systems to be developed not around categorical disabilities, such as mental illness, alcoholism, and mental retardation, but around human services as a whole. Separate departments of mental health, welfare, corrections, family services, and the like are being merged into unitary human service departments. This one-step "shopping center" idea as it is applied to human services is more consumer-oriented and, in reality, more holistic. It acknowledges the fact that human problems do not present themselves in neatly separate categories. A patient, or client, may have a whole variety of problems and may need what might better be termed human services rather than categorical services. Departments of health and social services in many states have already reorganized along these lines, as have many college and university departments relating to these disciplines. Whether service-oriented or academic, these departments have proliferated as an acknowledgment that this trend is, if not here to stay, then certainly likely to color the provision of human services for at least the next decade.

In this new human services setting, emphasis is placed on a generalist, rather than a specialist, as being at least the first person with whom the client comes in contact. This generalist is more likely to be a paraprofessional than a professional, and to have a liberal arts, rather than a specialized, background. This human services practitioner most likely functions as a case manager or treatment coordinator rather than as a therapist with a specific specialty. The position of case manager calls for a versatile generalist who is able to call on the services of the more highly skilled specialist when it is necessary to do so. Training for the case manager is likely to be at a bachelor's degree level, at an associate degree level, or perhaps even at a high school level. The case manager may well be a recovered drug abuser or a recovering alcoholic, whose laboratory of learning has been his or her own disability and encounter with the illness or disability itself. The credentialing process for such a practitioner employs a different mode from the traditional academic degree-granting mechanism. This proliferating generalist category of practitioners represents the most formidable (in terms of numbers) and challenging (in terms of creativity) teaching and training possibilities for educators.

Trends in Traditional Disciplines

The case manager coordinating treatment obviously needs someone to whom to refer persons who require more specialized services. The role of the discipline-oriented specialist, then, will not disappear. Rather, it changes to the extent that this more traditionally trained practitioner is not the first contact for the individual patient coming into the system. Like the medical specialist, this practitioner becomes a referral resource for the generalist.[1]

In spite of the proliferation of case managers, paraprofessionals, and generalists, there are still great numbers of specialists required to fill vacancies throughout the country. In 1978, for example, the National Institute of Mental Health (NIMH), after undertaking a telephone survey of professional mental health vacancies in state mental hospitals and community mental health service agencies in twenty states whose collective population comprised 34 percent of that of the United States, reported a total of 956 vacancies for psychiatrists, psychologists, psychiatric nurses, and social workers.[2] Based on this study and on extrapolations of its figures to the states not surveyed, current vacancies for professionally prepared psychiatrists, psychologists, psychiatric nurses, social workers, and other senior administrators and clinicians in state hospitals and community mental health services agencies total approximately 3,200.

This figure, large enough, may not represent the true number of vacancies. The boundaries of the system within which individuals receive diagnosis, care, and treatment for mental and emotional problems are diffuse, indistinct, and permeable. Unpublished calculations by NIMH indicate that the specialty mental health sector represented in its survey accounts for treatment of only a very small portion of individuals with mental disorders. In fact, state and county mental hospitals, along with psychiatric units of general hospitals and Veterans Administration hospitals, community mental health centers, and the practices of private psychiatrists and psychologists account for only 15 percent of mental health services. Roughly another 55 percent of mentally ill patients are seen in general medical primary care out-patient settings, such as offices of general practitioners, neighborhood mental health centers, industry-based health facilities, health department clinics and the out-patient services and emergency rooms of general hospitals. About 3 percent require the in-patient services of general hospitals or nursing homes; 6 percent are in a mixed mental health/out-patient medical setting, and the remaining roughly 20 percent either are receiving services in some other location in the general human services system or are not receiving any services at all.

In summary, there are approximately 3,200 vacancies nationwide for professionally prepared psychiatrists, psychologists, psychiatric nurses, and social workers in state hospitals and community mental health services agencies. Since these facilities account for only a very small portion of individuals being treated for mental disorders, it is very likely that professional-level vacancies are quite sizable. This situation can be expected to remain unchanged for a fairly long period of time.

Mental Health Delivery Systems

Within the human services network, a mental health delivery system will still exist, not as a stand-alone categorical entity but as part of the spectrum of human services to which the generalist can make referrals. Based on the findings of the President's Commission on Mental Health, established by Executive Order of the president in February 1977, President Jimmy Carter on October 7, 1980, signed into law a Mental Health Systems Act that is expected to color and shape psychiatry in the United States in the 1980s as significantly as the Community Mental Health Centers Act (CMHC) did in the 1960s.[3] This Mental Health Systems Act is undergirded by a new clinical manpower program to replace the thirty-year federal program of support for basic professional education.

Several significant trends are evident within the Mental Health Systems Act. First, "target services" is the new key phrase employed throughout the Mental Health Systems Act. Second, new initiatives, clinical manpower, and services are designed for those *target population groups* identified by the commission as being underserved, unserved, or inappropriately served. Funds will be distributed on a priority basis to those populations, underserved, unserved, or inappropriately served, such as chronic patients, severely disturbed children and adolescents, and the elderly. The manpower initiative would give traditional federal responsibilities to the state and divert money used for traditional professional training into specialized training for *targeted services*.

A third clear trend will be to replace a fifteen-year-old community mental health systems program, retaining its basic philosophy and goals, yet writing in a greater role for states in planning and operating mental health programs. More flexible start-up requirements for local grantees in shortage areas will be allowed. One of the clearly targeted services will be the chronically ill mental patient.

A fourth trend, with respect to manpower itself, will be to withdraw some support from the fundamental four "core" professions—

psychology, psychiatry, psychiatric nursing, and social work—and redirect money toward specialized training to answer specific needs of the targeted populations. Students receiving financial support from this program will be required to "pay back" the taxpayer by serving in an identified shortage area. Support would be rechanneled from basic education, special education, and research in the area of training specialists to work with children, adolescents, the elderly, minorities, and other underserved or unserved populations. Funds are expected to be allocated by service priority area rather than by discipline, although the four core disciplines would still be eligible for funds, provided universities can demonstrate that appropriate departments are specifically gearing training toward underserved populations. Some funds would still be allocated by discipline, but only for training programs in priority settings such as public agencies, rural areas, and inner cities; for developing training programs for primary care givers; and for developing methods to integrate specialty training with basic education.

The magic words in the Mental Health Systems Act are *targeted populations*, *targeted training*, and *targeted service delivery*. Pure training in a discipline is to be replaced with what is now called *targeted training*.

Holism and Specialization

In permeating the entire field of health care, the emphasis on holistic concepts and "wellness" has permeated the specific field of mental health care. As the physical health care system begins to view persons holistically, rather than categorically, and emphasizes health rather than illness, strengths rather than disabilities, and prevention rather than treatment, so too do these same themes color mental health programming. Accompanying this holistic movement is a trend toward specialization, or perhaps superspecialization. It may at first seem that these two trends—holism and specialization—are contradictory, or at least competitive. They are not, however, because behind the generalist must stand a specialist ready to vend a particular special service. This is equivalent to the trend in medicine; the era of the specialist has actually generated a new surge of interest in the family physician, the generalist. In medicine the health care system will come ultimately to reflect, then, a more balanced partnership between the specialist and generalist in which neither will dominate. The same can be expected in the field of mental health.

That specialization and holism developed side by side is an entirely understandable phenomenon. Two main dynamics contribute to it. No doubt some of the attraction to holistic views represents a reaction to the fragmentation, depersonalization, and myopia that specialization creates. Yet another contributing dynamic consists of the increasing complexity of, the growth of knowledge within, and the developing sophistication of the field of mental health. All of this is occurring at a rapid and even accelerating rate. As knowledge and technologies multiply, practitioners must narrow their expertise in order to be truly specialists. This produces more fragmentation, more myopia, and, necessarily, some depersonalization. It seems inevitable that one cannot be at the same time a good generalist and a good specialist. Hence, there is a complementary development of both. This mutual development is not a competition; both areas are noble endeavors.

In the mental health field certain areas of specialization, based on a knowledge explosion, are emerging. There is a general agreement, finally, that major mental illness such as schizophrenia, psychotic depressive reactions, and manic-depressive illness are biochemical disorders. Interest in and knowledge about brain biochemistry, a field that is really only twenty years old, has already produced wide superspecialization, and it is expected that psychopharmacology will become even more precise and specialized. While the brain mediates its activity chemically, it is basically an electrical device that happens to use chemical reactions to conduct its electrical business. On the heels of psychopharmacology will come—this is already happening—an intense interest in mediating brain activity directly, and doing so electrically. In the areas of epilepsy and certain kinds of spasticity, pacemakers are already in day-to-day clinical use. The brain pacemaker, in psychiatric as well as neurologic disorders, will likely become as commonplace as the heart pacemaker. The approach to mental illness in the future is likely to be electrical rather than chemical; a whole new technology has already developed and will dramatically proliferate.

Another area of inquiry already under way is in the area of sleep research and newer approaches to disorders of sleep as well as to other disorders of altered consciousness. Sleep laboratories and sleep specialists are now scattered throughout the United States, with many expect laboratories for newer approaches to appetite control—also a centrally determined function, just as sleep is—to become as commonplace as sleep laboratories. Biofeedback, another new branch of treatment, has spawned a virtual explosion in new machines, technicians to operate them, and clinicians to direct their use. The more highly specialized behavioral and psychotherapeutic techniques—such as implosive therapy, confrontation treatment, sexual counseling, progressive relaxation, family therapy, desensitization therapy, and Gestalt therapies, to name only a few—will also proliferate. Neurogenetics and the speciality of genetic counselor provide another area of interest with daily expanding sophistication and numbers of practitioners to carry out that area of subspecialization.

This discussion does not represent an exhaustive list of developing subspecialization in the field of mental health but points out only that such trends are occurring; whatever directions emerge, subspecialties have implications for professional educators. Just as educational opportunities must exist for the specialist in these highly sophisticated areas, so will such opportunities need to be available to the generalist. Holistic practitioners—experts in prevention and early nontraditional intervention—will be teachers in their own right, offering courses in wellness and holistic health. The holistic practitioner will be as much a health educator as a health practitioner, teaching "patients" about stress management, for example, or helping the "patient" to identify major transition points in the life cycle before they occur and to learn how to respond to these transition points. Just as interest in jogging as a technique for wellness has swept the United States, some type of psychological jogging techniques will rise as a counterpart, teaching us to jog mentally for wellness. Professional educators will need to accommodate their thinking toward the proliferation of wholeness and specialization as simultaneous but complementary, different but not competitive, concurrent trends.

Sane Asylums

As mentioned earlier, asylums, places of security and retreat, fell into disrepute because of underfunding. Patients were supposed to get away, but instead were put away. If people needed places of security and retreat a hundred years ago, it is apparent that such places are still needed now, albeit different populations and different purposes may be involved.

Psychiatrists regularly prescribe "asylums" for their patients, variously named a "rest in the hospital," a leave of absence, encounter weekends, sanatoria, camps, jet-away specials, Esalen, Synanon, Tassajara, rallies, crusades, and medical missions. But substantial problems exist with each of these approaches and alternatives. Some are extremely expensive. Others require considerable routinization and ritualization. Others require a specific "admission ticket," whether this be an illness, a crisis, an addition, a crime, a religion, a disadvantage, a certain sophistication, or a specific persuasion.

I propose that we reinstitute the asylum, and even call it that, as a place of "security and retreat" into which persons and their families may easily enter, checking in and out unashamedly, legitimately, noneuphemistically, without having to apologize, make excuses, borrow money, mortgage the home, take an oath, be baptized, or answer to peer review. I envision this asylum as a place remote, pastoral, modest, inexpensive, and away. No Joint Commission on Accreditation of Hospitals, no Utilization Review, no Tissue Committee. Persons entering would not be called patients, clients, subjects, inmates, or members; they would be called participants, and they would not be "admitted" but instead allowed simply to check in and check out, easily and informally. No computerized reservation system, no room service, no heated indoor pool.

The asylum would present a variety of possibilities, opportunities, and alternatives. Best of all, there would be other people there, people simply retreating and recharging. It would be a place where if one wanted to be involved in a group, one could be. If one wanted to run, or sit, or stare, or sing, one could do that. If one wanted to be unconventional, that would be okay too. There would be others to relate to, to share with, to talk to, and to be with. Or if one wanted simply to be alone and reflect, that would be all right also.

Activities would be available, but they would be optional. No recreational director, no tour guide, no prescribed therapies. Discussion groups, transactional analysis, transcendental meditation, yoga, lectures, experiential exercises, impromptu recitals, arts, crafts, work—whatever—would be there to become involved in or not depending on the participant's wishes. If one wanted to explore a predicament with another person and talk over problems, fine. If one wanted to collect oneself rather than explore oneself, that would be all right also. Confrontation and encounter or soliloquy and retreat would be equally valid and acceptable.

There already are some such places—hospitals, retreats, camps, foundations, and centers—that provide these elements. But there are substantial difficulties and shortcomings with many of these places. First, each of these places—and, most of all, hospitals—necessarily routinize, ritualize, and standardize the patient experience and thus destroy the essential spontaneity, individuality, and flexibility required in what I perceive as a true asylum. Second, in many of the available settings, various minimum standards, requirements, and codes mandate quantities of experienced staff and expensive facilities. My concept of an asylum, however, is a modest place without a myriad of highly trained treators descending on a cadre of helpless treatees; nor is it a posh place with wall-to-wall amusements and distractions. Rather, it is a simple site where the greatest helping resources are the very participants themselves, who, with a minimum of structure, serve as the main source of comfort, help, and hope for one another.

Third, as noted previously, most present-day asylums require some type of admission ticket. The admission ticket to this new type of asylum would be the simple acknowledgment of the very human need, every now and then, to step back, reflect, retreat, drop out (or even cop out, if you like) for a bit and to do so without stigma, without apology, and without rationalization. It would be an acknowledgment that each person reaches, every now and then, a private "I've had it" breaking point—a collective and common phenomenon that does not at all bespeak weakness, laziness, irresponsibility, or selfishness. The only admission ticket, then, is joint humanness and shared predicaments.

Psychiatric hospitals are needed, to be sure, by certain kinds of psychiatric patients who require intensive treatment. But if there were places people did not need a travel agent to get to and did not need to have an illness to qualify for, many, many people could avoid being hospitalized, could be kept from dropping out, or could be kept from killing themselves by work, by stress, or by their own hand.

Established psychiatric hospitals could be devoted to a dual use. In one portion of the hospital, the truly mentally ill person could be treated as a patient, and the usual and necessary rules, regulations, staffing patterns, and accreditation requirements would apply. As an alternative use, the remainder of the hospital, however, would become a sanctuary for what might be called the "worried well," who could, in that portion of the hospital, cop out for a bit from the numerous problems in living when those problems threaten to become overwhelming or overpowering. This would be a place to reflect, relate, be involved, and rest. The cost would not be great. (Average daily cost, not including professional expenses, in hospitals in the United States varies from area to area; it presently is approximately $150 to $200 per patient per day. Estimated cost, including professional expenses, for such a facility as described here would be $15 to $25 per day.) The procedures would be most uncumbersome, and the visit would remain unrecorded.

Such an asylum would be an entirely legitimate societal undertaking. Society already subsidizes a vast amount of resources in the form of hospitals, crisis centers, emergency rooms, detention homes, jails, halfway houses, and storefront clinics, each of which is really an alternative to the asylum. Why should society, then, not underwrite a facility that does not require quite so gigantic an admission ticket?—a place where the "worried well" could go before they become the "worried sick."

The impact on hospital admissions, family breakups, and even suicide with just a small investment might be large. But more than that, it would more honestly, more boldly, and more humbly acknowledge that each of us, at some point in life, has a private breaking point and a private need to retreat, recharge, and recoup.

The problems in living in 1974 sound familiar indeed: "Hopes once bright now dashed; ambitions which lure beyond strength; life's work begun but left unfinished; affections ripened only to be blasted." The modern-day version of these problems calls forth a very old remedy—an asylum. In order to gain public attention and in order to capture federal or foundation support, the idea of an asylum will need to be presented as a novel or new concept. The name will perhaps need to be changed to something more aesthetic, more mod, and more transcendental, perhaps some Greek or Latin term that means something or other and lends itself to some sort of logo.

But the basic purpose must remain unchanged.

In medicine and in psychiatry we revolve as we evolve.[4] We regularly rediscover as much as we newly discover, and the time is here, it seems to me, to rediscover and acknowledge a pressing need for a place of security and retreat for all of us from time to time that we may call, for lack of a better term, an asylum.

There are many reasons—economic, sociologic, logistic—why the sane asylum as I have described it is a viable alternative to the mental hospital as we know it. But the principal reason for its existence, as is our purpose, is that with a sane asylum, some in-patient experiences could be prevented, some tranquilizers could remain unprescribed, some substances could remain unabused, and some lives could be made more meaningful. These represent reason enough.

In summary, the field of mental health is full of emerging trends, all of which have implications for the professional educator. To the professional educator I would give the same advice I have used at my hospital in attempting to be attentive to new directions and innovative in new programming. As director of an institute, one of my duties is to help design new buildings, whenever we are fortunate enough to get funds for new construction. Artistically or architecturally, I have little to contribute to our building program, but I have, through the years, made a single, repetitive observation that has changed our building program rather dramatically. I noticed that whenever we completed a new building and installed our sidewalks where, according to our sidewalk consultants, they were supposed to be, and after we had put in expensive sod everywhere else, the people who used the new building told us by their paths over the sod where the sidewalks really ought to have been placed. So now, by executive order of the director, whenever we complete a new building here, we put sod all over the area surrounding the buildings, wait one year, see where the paths naturally develop, and then put the sidewalks over those paths. Our sidewalks, and our buildings, get much more use that way.

Part of being a good administrator, a good clinician, and a good educator is to be an observer of where the paths to and from our agencies and services are naturally developing and to be prepared to move our sidewalks to those paths rather than rigidly insist that people use the sidewalks that we have, through the years, developed. Rearranging our sidewalks to where they actually are, rather than to where we feel they ought to be, is an activity each of us, in our respective fields, must be prepared for. In an emerging and changing collage of mental health services, this is a particularly apt manner of observation and activity for the professional educator.

NOTES

1. Board of Trustees, Northern Hospital for the Insane, *Second Annual Report* (Oshkosh, Wis., September 30, 1974).
2. Center for State Mental Health Development, *Report to the Task Force on Manpower Policy* (Rockville, Md.: National Institute of Mental Health, May 5, 1978).
3. President's Commission on Mental Health, *Report to the President*, vol. 1 (Washington, D.C.: U. S. Government Printing Office, 1978).
4. Darold A. Treffert, "Psychiatry Revolves as It Evolves," *Archives of General Psychiatry* 17 (July 1967):72-74.

8

Trends in Youth Service Organizations

Robert V. Carlson

INTRODUCTION

General Observations

Opportunities for professionals interested in serving the needs of youth are linked irrevocably to our society's view of youth. This chapter examines our prevailing attitudes toward youth and the implications of these attitudes for the professionals who serve them. Specifically presented in this chapter are the following perspectives:

1. Youth services presently being provided are fragmented, insufficient, and inherently controversial.

2. There is a dearth of research and a general neglect concerning the identification of youth's needs and the design of youth service delivery systems.

3. There are trends that, even though limited, suggest some recognition of the unique developmental needs of youth.

The author wishes to acknowledge the contribution of the study by Joan Lipsitz, *Growing Up Forgotten: A Review of Research and Programs Concerning Early Adolescence* (Lexington, Mass.: D.C. Heath and Co., 1977), to the development of this chapter.

In addition, this chapter provides an overview of potential professional opportunities and outlines the implications of emerging trends for the professional preparation of youth-serving personnel.

Definitions

To appreciate fully our society's present confusion concerning youth and the concomitant provision of youth services, an examination of alternative definitions of youth seems in order. This review is pertinent to understanding the complexities of identifying a target population to serve, the arbitrariness often associated with limiting the scope of services, and the fragmentation ensuing from policies that are often based on political expediency. This review is not intended to be exhaustive, but to be sufficient to make persons interested in youth services sensitive to the importance of defining the service population from as clear a perspective as possible.

To understand the interrelationship of terms used to describe our young citizens, explication of *youth* as a generic concept is a place to start. James Coleman argues that our present practice of extending the dependency of young people suggests the need to define *youth* as embracing the ages of fourteen to twenty-four. His point is that many factors—including insufficient employment opportunities, encouraged participation in higher education, and delayed marriages—lead an increased number of young people to maintain up through the age of twenty-four some degree of financial dependence on their parents or guardians.[1] Thus, to limit the scope of concern to youths fourteen to eighteen years old would be to overlook a cluster of young people who have not acquired full independence and who continue to acquire knowledge and understanding of their development into adulthood.

Adolescence is seen as a subset of youth usually spanning the age period of fourteen to eighteen, although Joan Lipsitz notes that from a biological standpoint adolescence spans the period between the "onset of puberty and the completion of bone growth."[2] As Hans Sebald indicates, adolescence means "to grow up" or "to grow into maturity." He further states that from a "sociological sense [adolescence] is a means of passing through the unstructured and ill-defined phase that lies between childhood and adulthood."[3] Sebald is not necessarily in conflict with Coleman's definition of youth since many do not acquire adulthood until age twenty-four or later; also, his sense of adolescence does not preclude individuals from taking on adult responsibilities at a much earlier age.

The term *juvenile* seems reserved for youth who have not reached legal maturity set by 1971 federal legislation as age eighteen and who have violated the law or who are "status offenders," that is, have violated certain youth-related restrictions of their state or community such as breaking curfew, drinking in a bar, or purchasing cigarettes. Thus, services provided a juvenile tend to be of a legal nature involving the police, courts, corrections, and related organizations.

Terms such as *teenager, young adult, young radical, student, older adolescents*, and others are often used interchangeably and may often reflect or connote a certain attitude or belief about youth. There appear to be strongly held values about youth, and some of these terms become a shorthand for expressing such values. The danger in labeling, particularly in using negative labels, is that of initiating and reinforcing a self-fulfilling prophecy.

In its report on youth policy needs the Center for Action Research in Washington, D.C., stated: "When parents, teachers, and friends all begin to use labels as a basis for their interaction with a person, the individual is under great pressure to define himself in a similar way and to behave in a way which is consistent with this definition."[4]

This chapter attempts to address the broadest spectrum and orientation of youth, not only from a chronological perspective but also from an interdisciplinary perspective. The intent is not to limit our review to a narrow age range nor to approach youth from a single focus. In order to appreciate fully the breadth of services they require, youth should be viewed holistically. Their needs should be examined from psychological, legal, biological, and other perspectives. Each orientation and combination of orientations can provide a perspective concerning an individual's acquisition of adulthood. Our American culture continues to refine its expectations for each aspect of youth development, which enables us to draw a distinction between youth and adulthood. Other societies have resolved by very programmatic means the problem of determining the point at which an individual achieves adulthood. For example, in some societies a male is a full adult only after he has a full-grown son. In rural Greece, a young man spends about ten years arranging his sisters' dowries before he is considered a man. Among the Irish, a son is not a mature adult until his father retires.

Sebald offers a comprehensive framework for determining the termination of adolescence:

1. Sociologically, the termination of status discontinuity

2. Psychologically, completing a number of developmental tasks and achieving a modicum of consistent identity

3. Biologically, achieving physiological maturity

4. Legally, reaching the age limit specified by law

5. Economically, becoming self-supporting and maintaining a balance between production and consumption

6. Traditionally, when informal customs lift the last restrictions on adult privileges.[5]

Although Sebald's holistic framework is comprehensive, it does not ease the confusion as to where the stage of youth begins. Most experts seem to agree that youth begins with the onset of puberty, which, however, is not necessarily a stable phenomenon and has been changing over a period of time. Ann Peterson writes:

> In Norway, the average girl begins to menstruate at just over 13 years of age, as opposed to 17 years in the late 1840s. In the United States where children mature up to a year earlier than in European countries the average age at first menstruation has declined from 14.2 in 1900 to about 12.45 today. According to British pediatrician J.M. Tanner, who has compiled statistics on the subject, the age at menarche has declined an average of four months per decade for the past century. [6]

Peterson indicates that earlier and earlier maturation will eventually "level off when people are nourished at an optimal level."[7]

It is equally confusing to determine precisely where youth ends and adulthood begins. As outlined above, Sebald offers several dimensions on which to make this determination, but due to the complexity of these factors a specific age level is impossible to ascertain for all youth. Therefore, it seems that any attempt to delimit youth services to a particular age range is somewhat arbitrary and based on convenience. For our purposes, the years from twelve to twenty-four do not appear unreasonable since this period of time appears sufficiently unique when contrasted with other stages of life to be acceptable for defining *youth*.

Historical Perspective

It is also interesting to examine the shifts in perceptions of youth in our society. Coleman speaks of three societal phases and their effects upon youth. He identifies phase one as being agrarian-focused, which brought youth onto the labor scene, particularly on the farm, at an early age. As our society began to feel the impact of industrialization, it moved into a schooling phase, wherein youth were kept off the labor market in order to increase their potential for productivity. Finally, we are entering a third phase, one that recognizes the importance not only of cognitive development of youth but also other aspects of their lives as well. Coleman stresses the importance for youth to develop a number of aspects of their lives: "Beyond the acquisition of marketable skills one needs to develop a capability of effective management of one's own affairs and develop capabilities as a consumer, not only in reference to goods but also the cultural riches of civilization."[8]

Important legal shifts have also occurred. In 1899, the desire emerged to separate youth from adults in terms of judging illegal acts and related incarceration or punishment. Legal judgments went beyond determining guilt to consider what would be in the best interest of the child and the state in order "to save him [the child] from a downward career."[9] Trends emphasizing the treatment and rehabilitation of child offenders and legal proceedings that were considered civil and not criminal and that entitled the child to "custody" were prominent during the early 1900s. Unfortunately, these noble gestures on behalf of youth had negative as well as positive consequences. Due to the special treatment desired for youth, legal precedent and related guidelines were lacking. As the Supreme Court observed in the *Gault* decision (1967): "Absence of procedural rules based on constitutional principle has not always produced fair, efficient, and effective procedures."[10] In the *Gault* decision, the Supreme Court ruled that youth need to be protected from abrogations of their basic rights and not be subject to extended imprisonment for committing illegal acts that often go unpunished when committed by adults. The *Gault* decision has become a landmark case in ensuring that youth have the full benefit and protection of the law.

Our sense of the role youth should play in our society as well as our attitude toward youth continue to reflect ambivalence. We have vacillated between treating youth as young adults so they could provide skilled labor on farms and in the early factories and treating them as children who require protection from the evils and dangers of adult society. When our sensibilities became peaked by horrid incidents of youthful exploitation and cruel treatment by our legal systems, then a more protective attitude toward the young developed.

The legacies of these past practices still exist, and a paradox has emerged in our treatment of youth. Due to technological advances requiring better educated—but fewer—workers, youth have been encouraged to remain in school. The study by Jerald Bachman and his colleagues of the school dropout problem illustrates how a well-meaning effort can have deleterious effects. Certain young people stay in school primarily because they do not want to be viewed as misfits; in school, they strain the capabilities of their institution to serve adequately the diverse needs of all its students.[11] The consequence has been a prolonged period in which young people depend upon the varying societal institutions through which they must pass. Such dependence continues to challenge these institutions as to how best to respond.

PRESENT STATE OF YOUTH SERVICES

The confusion as to how youth is to be defined and the equally confused state of our society as to what our attitude toward youth should be seem to have had their effects on our social institutions. Schools and human service agencies tend to mirror the society and reflect both its positive and negative attributes. This condition provides a backdrop and partial explanation for the first observation presented in this chapter, which is that the services provided for youth are fragmented, insufficient, and inherently controversial.

Fragmentation

As Lipsitz states:

> Social institutions that serve young adolescents can be no more coherent than the purposes that undergird them. Unsure of who these young adolescents are, unsure of ways in which other domains affect their lives, unsure of who we want these young people to be, we lack as a society the integrative purposefulness needed to provide for them coherently.[12]

Her careful analysis concludes that the various institutions attempting to address the needs of American youth—including the schools, the various service institutions for the handicapped and family, voluntary youth-serving agencies, and the juvenile justice system—

operate within fixed service boundaries and usually cope with adolescents in a vacuum.

A similar conclusion is reported in *Services for Handicapped Youth: A Program Overview*, which speaks to the "bewildering maze" of agencies, services, and programs for handicapped youth. This report identifies problems in five major categories: (1) inequity, (2) gaps in services, (3) insufficient knowledge, (4) inadequate or deficient control, and (5) insufficiency of resources. With regard to inadequate control the report points out that "no one individual or group of individuals plans, monitors, or controls the handicapped service system."[13] This problem does not seem unique to services for handicapped youth but reflects deficiencies in youth services in general. In response to the problem, the Center for Action Research report calls for a national strategy to enable "youth to become useful, productive, and contributing adults in their communities"[14] by changing community social institutions rather than the behavior of individual youth. Recognizing the need to counter fragmentation, the Center offers a plan "for local governments to define and to cultivate a youth services system—a network of relationships among youth serving organizations—which would be capable of a coherent, coordinated and comprehensive approach to the problems of youth."[15]

Insufficiency

Up to the present, schools—particularly public-supported institutions—have been and no doubt will continue to be the major institution influencing youth development. Compulsory school attendance laws and the raising of high school graduation requirements will continue to pressure youth to remain in schools. This places upon the schools high expectations that have yet to be accommodated. As Coleman argues:

> The school system, as now constituted, offers an incomplete context for the accomplishment of many important facets of maturation. The school has been well designed to provide some kinds of training but, by virtue of that fact, is inherently ill-suited to fulfill other tasks essential to the creation of adults. Indeed, it would be unreasonable to expect any institution to suffice as the exclusive environment for youth. Signs of dissatisfaction abound, from parents and taxpayers who have an inarticulate sense that something is amiss, from school administrators and teachers who are experimenting with methods and objectives and forms that differ from those of the established system, and from youth themselves, many of whom are showing individual initiative in the search for extracurricular experiences.[16]

Essentially, Coleman and others are saying that the needs of youth are sufficiently complex and too comprehensive for single-purpose institutions such as schools to be able to provide the breadth of opportunities deemed desirable and necessary. Schools are presently ill-designed to accomplish their broad and enormous charge.

Partly owing to the limitations and failures of public schools there has arisen in the past decade an alternative school movement. Alternative schools, however, have not been fully successful in filling the gaps. Unfortunately, these institutions have a short life span, less than two years on the average. In addition, they have been plagued by boredom and frustration stemming from seemingly endless discussions about the breakdowns in organizational routine. Often these schools have been characterized as "corridors of wandering souls." Coleman writes:

> Recent efforts to establish a new variety in American secondary education have not gotten very far. Their support has been hesitant and uneven. The new starts that center on work or job training have to solve the dumping-ground problem. The new places for disaffected affluent youth have been deficient in such minimal requirements of organization as a capacity to set goals, divide the labor, and delegate authority. [17]

Although schools are frequently able to provide an environment that meets the needs of the young, studies do point out areas that need to be addressed. In her review of research concerning the developmental needs of youth, Lipsitz commented on the following points:

1. In regard to nutrition, a ten-state study found that youth between the ages of ten and sixteen have the highest rates of unsatisfactory nutritional status problems, including underweight, undersize, obesity, iron deficiency anemia, and dental caries.[18]

2. Literacy surveys conducted by the U.S. Department of Health, Education, and Welfare report that "approximately 4.8 percent, or 1 million of the 22.7 million youngsters who would be in grades six through twelve, cannot read materials for a fourth grader, that is, cannot read at the beginning fourth-grade level."[19] The literacy rate of adolescents was cited as an indicator of a nation at risk in the recent report issued by the National Commission on Excellence in Education. The fact that 13 percent of all 17-year-olds in the United States are considered functionally illiterate (and the

rate is much higher among minority youth) suggests there still is a real need. [20]

3. The mere number of handicapped youth indicates a sizable problem. Estimates suggest young people suffering significant physical or mental impairment numbered over 9 million in 1970, or approximately between 9 and 10 percent of the school-age population.[21] The actual number of handicapped young people may be as high as 12 percent with some variance across states.[22]

4. Sex-related problems (ranging from unwanted teenage pregnancies to uninformed distortion of the role of sex in a normal life), teenage depression, suicide, and drug and alcohol abuse are well documented and continue to place a heavy demand for appropriate services. [23]

5. Mentally handicapped youth, including mentally retarded (2.5 million in 1970) and learning disabled youngsters are part of the school-age youth in need of special education.

6. A Rand Corporation report estimated that of all handicapped youngsters in need of special education (about 9 percent of the school-age group), only 59 percent receive such services.[24] Although the percentage of handicapped young people served has increased since the passage of P.L. 94–142, not all individuals are receiving the services required by the law.[25]

7. Juvenile delinquency continues to pose a major challenge to our legal and enforcement systems. Self-report studies reveal that "up to 90 percent of all young people have committed acts that could bring them into the web of the juvenile justice system."[26] Another alarming statistic illustrating the magnitude of this problem is the following: "Although the mean age of onset for all white offenders was 14.2 and for nonwhite offenders 13.3, the mean age of onset for *chronic* offenders was approximately two years lower (12.0 for white and 11.6 for nonwhite)."[27]

In sum, in spite of the lack of any coordinated and continuous research concerning the needs and/or problems of young people, there are sufficient data and related observations to suggest that a wide range of services are required. The Center for Action Research suggests that youth development happens in spite of coordinated plans or programs. However, little money is allocated for prevention with billions spent "annually on arresting, rearresting, supporting, treating, and trying to patch up" each new batch of youth that runs into obstacles.[28]

Current systems designed to meet the pressing needs of prevention are falling short. The Rand Corporation report generally concluded that there is neglect and underdevelopment of both preventive services and effective methods of referral. The report points out that "agencies are not serving a significant portion of those who have a need, do not know who are unserved, and do not have outreach programs."[29]

An example of this situation is the juvenile justice system. Lipsitz indicates that those holding informed but divergent points of view nevertheless do

> agree on one point: the juvenile system is a failure as it now functions. . . . The burden placed on the juvenile justice system is unwieldy. In short, the role of the court permits interference in the lives of young people, whether or not they have committed a crime, promises to "cure" them, and is not required to allow them the opportunity to refuse treatment. Theoretically, it is responsible for the rehabilitation of over 1 million adolescents annually.[30]

These failings are mainly due to lack of manpower resources and knowledge of effective ways of handling youth cases. In addition, the institutions to which youth are referred are overcrowded and understaffed and lack sufficient alternatives for rehabilitation.

In 1979, the American Bar Association ratified "a set of standards based on the theory that since the juvenile court cannot remake children in an ideal image, and indeed since it often makes their troubled lives worse for the attempt, it should stop trying."[31] The standards reflect a more pragmatic view toward the treatment of juvenile delinquents.

According to Lipsitz: "The lack of options for young adolescents became a recurrent theme. . . . It has its counterpoint in the lack of alternatives in training for youth workers, including teachers."[32] The present state of youth services presents to individuals and institutions, including higher education, a significant challenge to examine and research issues, disseminate information, and prepare qualified persons to ameliorate present deficiencies.

The description of the present state of services has its corollary when it comes to accumulated knowledge generated by research and evaluation studies. A review of such studies also presents a general picture of fragmentation and insufficiency. Some observations suggesting the nature of the situation are as follows:

1. Based on a review of over 6,600 pertinent abstracts and contact with more than 200 agencies and institutes, there is evidence that very little quality evaluation of prevention programs is being funded. In 1970, $11.5 billion was spent on prevention programs, but 57 percent of those programs had no evaluations.[33]

2. Research addressing specific long-term concerns of youth is nonexistent. Rather, there is "a hodgepodge of ad hoc research on family size, sibling relationships, single parent and typical family groupings, working mothers, family background, family and peer orientations and parenting styles. None of these focuses specifically on the early adolescent."[34]

3. There is little literature on the development of handicapped adolescents. In the prestigious two volumes of *Issues in the Classification of Children*, Lipsitz found only one article in the literature not about delinquency that concerns adolescents and takes a developmental perspective.[35]

4. There is a lack of concentrated or appreciable research in reference to adolescent development. As John Hill observed: "There are few areas in which investigations relating to the key issues of adolescence have moved beyond exploratory efforts and clinically based theoretical formulations."[36]

Other research gaps concerning the development of youth include such areas as the meaning of the earlier onset of puberty and, more importantly, the impact of puberty upon the development of youth; the variability of development of and within various age groups and the impact of such variability on institutional policies and practices; and the need for keeping research current, given the continued changes occurring in youth development.

Hill and the Social Research Group suggest specific research issues or questions worthy of systematic review. Taken together, these issues indicate a call for basic programmatic research and evaluation that relate very directly with emerging conditions of youth and a need to develop policies and programs that are relevant, current, and data-based. In addition, Hill calls for better-prepared youth workers.[37] To put it another way: "Numbers of young Americans have evolved into a new class of native aliens."[38] Can we seize the moment, redirect and focus research and evaluation efforts in some coordinated and concentrated manner so that future and present youth workers can develop programs that match the needs of their clientele? A sizable change is called for.

In spite of the portrayals of despair and shortfalls, some current events suggest emerging trends that provide a positive perspective on future directions of institutions serving youth and on related employment opportunities for future youth workers, including teachers.

There will certainly continue to be a pressing need for qualified persons to meet the needs of youth, particularly of handicapped youth, within our current educational systems. Thus, when surveying future opportunities, expanded services within education must be considered a viable option. In addition to school-based trends, there are movements that interface with schools, for example, in juvenile justice systems, that should provide opportunities for professional employment. Finally, there are organizations and related situations outside education that presently require, and no doubt in the future will continue to require, better-trained persons to provide educationally related services to youth in a variety of settings.

School-Based

In spite of continued problems and frustrations associated with our public schools, particularly at the secondary level, there does not appear to be a concerted effort to dismantle the system. In the 1960s we experienced attempts by the Office of Economic Opportunity and the alternative or free school movement to establish educational opportunities outside public schools. For various reasons these efforts have either ceased to exist or have been reduced in number. Even the pressure for school integration and busing have not resulted in the large-scale proliferation of private schools that many predicted or anticipated. This is not to suggest that public schools are not without their faults or limitations but rather that the resources and energy to create and continue other options are quite demanding and difficult to sustain.

From the public school perspective, the trend of mainstreaming or the principle of placement in the least restrictive environment has, no doubt, the greatest potential in the foreseeable future for altering practices in schools and for creating additional opportunities. The thrust of new legislation, particularly P.L. 94–142, is designed to provide instruction for handicapped pupils in the most appropriate environment. Currently this mandate is being translated into reducing the amount of time spent by such pupils in separate special education classrooms. The goal is to place children who have learning needs and handicapping conditions into regular classrooms, whenever and wherever feasible.

The practices to meet the intent of this mainstreaming legislation are still emerging, but it is reasonable to expect that a greater emphasis on individualization of instruction will result, provided that the legislation remains in effect and allocations keep pace with its demand. Present regulations require developing an Individual Educational Plan (IEP) for each child identified as having a special need. The nature of the regular classroom may change significantly, with teachers working less with large groups and providing instructional patterns that include more small-group and individual teaching. It is possible that parents of nonhandicapped students may demand that all students have IEPs. The number of employed professional staff (464,200 as of 1970) will not be sufficient to address this new direction, given the focus of the legislation and accompanying regulations. In fact, of the total handicapped pupils identified in 1970, nearly 42 percent did not receive designated types of instruction or assistance. The percentages of hearing-impaired, crippled, and partially sighted children receiving services ranged from 63 percent to 73 percent.[39] As can be inferred, we are in a catch-up mode to begin with, and the new legislation will no doubt create more pressure for additional services. Moreover, the spillover effect of focusing more on the needs of the individual child, who may or may not have a handicapping condition, should provide additional opportunities for instructional and support services staff.

Another trend, the concept of the community school, has grown out of a desire to establish closer relationships between the community and its schools, particularly its middle, junior high, and/or high schools. Allan Green of the Educational Facilities Laboratory speaks of a community school or center that "combines schools with other services, like recreation, day care, the arts, libraries, health, and job training."[40] If this trend does materialize, new opportunities should emerge where few exist now. For example, coordinating such services requires a clearer identification of gaps and the input of managerial skills. School personnel will no doubt require special preparation to establish competencies in these areas.

In addition to mainstreaming, the catch-up necessary for special needs of pupils, and the attention to such organizational structures as the community school, there is the concern for acquisition of basic knowledge or competency by pupils graduating from the public schools. Each of these trends functions independently to some degree, but together they suggest a common theme, a desire for a clearer articulation by the public, by legislatures, and by the courts as to what individuals or various interest groups desire and demand of their schools. This means, in effect, that the educational enterprise is viewed by many as being in the best position to increase learning opportunities for our young people regardless of the nature of the learner, his or her background or special need, and the limits of local resources.

Related Nonschool-Based

It would be inappropriate to limit the definition of opportunities or trends to school-based organizations. It is evident that our schools cannot possibly meet all the needs of developing youth. On the other hand, it is not likely that other institutions can or should operate in a vacuum separated from public schools.

The Center for Action Research attempts to speak to the complexity of youth needs and the need for coordination of youth services. The Center points out that a major need of youth is to develop a sense of legitimate identity and, thus, build a stake in conformity. Young people do and will see the merit of conforming to reasonable standards of behavior as they develop a greater sense of confidence, usefulness, sense of belonging, and power or potency. The Center suggests that these attributes are derived from experience in the work world and by participation in politics, in the family, and in recreational and cultural activities.[41] Certainly schools can contribute to the development of such attributes in young people, but effective interaction between schools and other institutions should provide a more comprehensive base for youth's development. Coleman summarizes the situation well:

> Schools are the principal formal institutions of society intended to bring youth into adulthood. But schools' structures are designed wholly for self-development, particularly the acquisition of cognitive skills and of knowledge. At their best, schools equip students with cognitive and noncognitive skills relevant to their occupational futures, with knowledge of some portion of civilization's cultural heritage, and with the taste for acquiring more such skills and knowledge. They do not provide extensive opportunity for managing one's affairs, they seldom encourage intense concentration on a single acitivity, and they are inappropriate settings for nearly all objectives involving responsibilities that affect others. Insofar as these other objectives are important for the transition to adulthood, and we believe they are, schools act to retard youth in this transition, by monopolizing their time for the narrow objectives that schools have.[42]

Coleman indicates several changes that would be desirable for youth: (1) creating departments concentrating on music, performing arts, science, physical education, and the crafts; (2) permitting young people to be brought into the work setting sooner; (3) establishing youth organizations and communities that provide opportunities for experiencing leadership roles, responsibilities, and self-management; (4) establishing a voucher system for youth at age sixteen, usable for training or education from that point on; and (5) providing opportunities for public service through a youth service corps. It is very unlikely that these developments will all occur, but they are reflective of the kinds of opportunities that are needed and were presented in a responsible way by the Panel on Youth for the President's Science Advisory Committee.[43] If, by some miracle of governmental policy, programs to meet these needs were identified and funded, the call for specially prepared youth service providers to work in such innovative areas would be significant and challenging.

Another emerging trend that will no doubt have an impact on schools in a variety of ways involves the changes presently occurring in the juvenile justice system. Beginning with the *Gault* decision in 1967, which placed some restrictions on the justice system in litigation involving youthful offenders, and with the Delinquency Prevention

Act of 1974 and its subsequent myriad amendments, significant shifts in dealing with youth are being implemented.

The Juvenile Justice and Delinquency Prevention Act of 1974 was passed "to assist local education agencies and other public and nonprofit private agencies to establish and carry out community-based programs, including programs in schools for prevention of delinquency in youths."[44] Part of the charge in the Act speaks to the necessary coordination of welfare, education, health, mental health, recreation, job training, job placement, corrections, and other related units. This federal law is developing into a significant piece of legislation, with an authorized appropriation of $150 million in fiscal year 1978 to $200 million in fiscal year 1980.[45]

As a result of this federal legislation, states are developing alternative proposals to deinstitutionalize youthful offenders and design alternative systems for meeting their needs. In the state of Vermont, for example, plans are being implemented to close the state's facility for youthful offenders and to develop arrangements for a continuum of care, from a stress on prevention at the local community level to a highly restricted program at the state level for more difficult youth cases. (See Figure 1 for a portrayal of the various components of and options within this new system.) This type of system represents an attempt to divert youth to institutions designed to address the specific nature of a youth problem and to place a heavier emphasis on prevention and rehabilitation at the community level where the youth reside. The success of such endeavors will depend to some degree upon persons with knowledge and understanding of the needs of youth and the educational process. These persons also need the ability to work between and among several institutions in order to maximize the forces available to the best interest of both the young person and his or her community. The net effect of these proposed changes is the creation of youth bureau operations requiring persons with professional status to bridge the gap between the needs of the youthful offender and the numerous support services.

Other Agencies

A variety of youth-serving agencies provide other opportunities for employment. The list below provides a sampling of such agencies.

1. *Boy Scouts of America and Girl Scouts of America.* Staff are primarily involved in recruiting and training volunteers, but Lipsitz makes

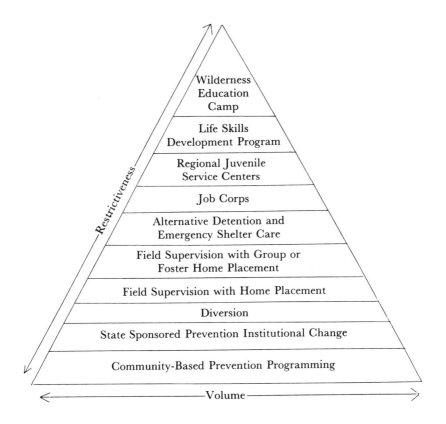

Figure 1.
Continuum of Care in Vermont's Reorganized
Juvenile Justice System

an interesting observation about the Scouts: "The problem is that these older institutions fail to fulfill an important need of youth, to feel that they have a function in the initiation, development, and execution of activities. The ritual ceremony and paramilitary structure are no longer enough to attract new membership, particularly in urban areas. In 1970, membership in the BSA was 6,183,086, and in the GSA, 3,920,000."[46] In 1983, the Boy Scouts reported having 3,567,214 members and the Girl Scouts 2,247,000.

2. *Young Men's Christian Association and Young Women's Christian Association.* The Y's professional staff, as opposed to volunteers, basically provide social, educational, and recreational programs for youth.

3. *Church-Related Organizations.* Such units as the B'nai B'rith Youth Organization, Young Men's and Women's Hebrew Association, Jewish Community Centers, and the Catholic Youth Organization provide social, educational, and recreational programs for youth.

4. *4H.* A national program operated through the auspices of the Cooperative Extension Services of the U.S. Department of Agriculture, 4H clubs operate in both rural and urban settings, provide an occupation-oriented program, and give instruction to youth for their future economic roles.

5. *National Federation of Settlements and Neighborhood Centers.* These basically urban-focused, neighborhood-based, and sometimes religiously oriented centers attempt to work with youth, their families, and the problems of their neighborhood.

6. *Save the Children Foundation.* A rural-focused organization, the foundation serves the disadvantaged by attempting to integrate the family unit and the community.

7. *Boys' and Girls' Clubs of America.* These are usually located in urban settings and provide social and recreational programs for youth.

8. *Coordinating Agencies.* Examples include Youth Service Bureaus, recommended by the President's Commission on Law Enforcement to handle troubled youth outside the criminal justice systems; the National Commission on Resources for Youth, which exists to promote models of programs in which youth can assume a high degree of responsibility; and the National Youth Alternatives Project, which acts as a clearinghouse for alternative youth programs. These organizations attempt to cross over many organizational jurisdictions and create lines of communication among various youth service agencies.

These groups represent just a small sampling of organizations that deal with youth in some direct way. In 1971 the President's Council on Youth Opportunity developed a *Youth Resources Manual,* which provides a comprehensive list of organizations, programs, and resource people.[47]

There is one cautionary and challenging observation to be made concerning such existing and future organizations wishing to serve youth. The statistics reported on the membership in the Scout organizations may be a harbinger of the future unless these organizations can adjust or alter their methods. As a result of her research, Gisela Konopka recommends:

1. Allowing adolescents to participate actively in planning and executing youth projects

2. Furnishing opportunities for adolescents to discuss their problems

3. Establishing co-ed activities

4. Reducing organizational structure to leave groups small, informal, and fairly autonomous

5. Active recruiting of "youth in trouble"

6. Encouraging significant participation in the public life of the community. [48]

Again, the challenge is before us to recognize the special needs of youth, expand their options, and provide well-qualified personnel to address those needs in a competent manner.

IMPLICATIONS OF TRENDS FOR PROFESSIONAL PREPARATION

In the field of education there is clearly some catching up to do in meeting the learning needs of handicapped youth both in and out of school. What is not altogether clear is what, if anything, can be done to prepare youth service professionals so as to fill the voids and reduce the fragmentation in services for youth. There are some overriding concerns suggested by this review, but they are not easily answered. Foremost in mind is to what end should youth services serve? Is it actively to ensure a quality life-style at a certain income free of life's stresses, abuses, and inconsistencies? Or is it to wait quietly, as a repairman, to be called upon to clarify, facilitate, and create conditions that youth seek at a particular time? Is it perhaps somewhere between these extremes at a point where problems, concerns, and needs of youth are anticipated and examined and reasonable alternatives that enable youth to discover their own potency are explored?

These choices point up our confusion regarding the nature of the purpose for which youth shall be served.

Another touchstone that has implications for training of the youth professional is the need for holistic theory, one that sees youth as a whole person, complex, and in need of understanding of his or her diversity or uniqueness. Such a theory must allow for the examination of the various aspects of youth needs, but it must also develop into a comprehensive theory that puts the parts together. It has been said that the human mind can handle only a limited number of variables simultaneously; thus by nature the human mind is precluded from fully comprehending the complexity of human nature. How can we begin to develop theories of human behavior that can appreciate, describe, and utilize a broad range of insights and lead to some guiding principles that deal with the total person?

Finally, there appears to be a need to keep our attention on our objective and not to overemphasize the means. That is, institutional or professional loyalties can make us lose sight of why our institutions and professions exist. There is a danger in overemphasizing the special nature of the field of education, or of social work, or of recreation, or of health services, and forgetting that each of these divisions has a common purpose for existing, that of serving the total needs of youth. One set of needs cannot be emphasized at the expense of another. "Youth" should serve as a unifying theme through which multiple institutions and professional identities can be identified and utilized in an integrated way.

This brings us to examine more closely what generic knowledge or skills seem essential to identifying appropriate goals on behalf of youth and to treating youth as whole persons, thus placing professional specialization second to the developmental needs of youth.

It is not difficult to conjure up a rather extensive list of competencies that transcend the boundaries of specific disciplines since experts have different opinions on this matter. What is suggested here are those analytical, conceptual, and interpersonal capabilities that would ideally supplement such specialized knowledge areas as education, health, criminal justice, and the like and that would also serve the three broad needs of clarifying the purposes served by youth services, devising strategies for working on the gestalt of need, and emphasizing client needs above parochial professional interests.

Some items that logically fall into these categories are as follows:

Analytical Theories
General systems theory
Political theory
Organizational theory
Youth development theory
Community development theory

Conceptual Strategies
Systems analysis and planning strategies
Program evaluation strategies
Pedagogical strategies
Youth services delivery strategies
Integration of services strategies
Needs assessment strategies

Interpersonal Skills
Counseling skills
Communication skills
Helping skills
Organizing and planning skills
Group dynamics skills
Conflict resolution skills

This list is not intended to be exhaustive but rather to provide stimulation for a continuing exchange that explores the contrast between generic and specialized competencies.[49]

A final question facing youth services is where best can these generic competencies be developed and taught to budding and practicing professionals. Eventually, some lines of responsibility will need to be drawn to ensure that youth become a strong focus for professional preparation and that supplementary specialized skills be pursued in appropriate subunits. One can dream of a coalition within an interdisciplinary unit consisting of education, social work, social services, health, and others, but the track record of higher education in sustaining interdisciplinary units reveals limited success. Be that as it may, a leadership vacuum appears to exist, and by virtue of their long-term commitments and involvements with youth, colleges of education are in an advantageous position to encourage further efforts in this direction. The youth of tomorrow may be better served than youth in the past if only the adults of the present can model an integrated system of preparation for youth service professionals. This challenge is still before us.

NOTES

1. James S. Coleman, *Youth: Transition to Adulthood* (Chicago: University of Chicago Press, 1974), pt. 2.
2. Joan Lipsitz, *Growing Up Forgotten* (Lexington, Mass.: D. C. Heath and Co., 1977), p. 3.
3. Hans Sebald, *Adolescence: A Social Psychological Analysis* (Englewood Cliffs, N.J.: Prentice-Hall, 1977), p.4.
4. Center for Action Research, *A Design for Youth Development Policy* (Washington, D.C.: Office of Youth Development, U.S. Department of Health, Education, and Welfare, 1976), p. 37.
5. Sebald, *Adolescence: A Social Psychological Analysis,* pp. 7-8.
6. Ann C. Petersen, "Can Puberty Come Any Earlier?" *Psychology Today* 12 (February 1979): 45.
7. Ibid.
8. Coleman, *Youth: Transition to Adulthood,* pp. 3-4.
9. Julian Mack, "The Juvenile Court," *Harvard Law Review* 23 (1909): 120.
10. *In Re Gault,* 387 U.S. 18 (1967).
11. Jerald G. Bachman, Swayzer Green, and Ilona D. Wirtanen, *Youth in Transition,* Vol. 3, *Dropping Out: Problem or Symptom?* (Ann Arbor, Mich.: Institute for Social Research, 1971).
12. Lipsitz, *Growing Up Forgotten,* p. 82.
13. James S. Kakalik, Garry D. Brewer, Laurence A. Dougharty, Patricia D. Fleishauer, and Samuel M. Genensky, *Services for Handicapped Youth: A Program Overview,* Report R–1220 (Santa Monica: Rand Corporation, 1973), p. 22.
14. Center for Action Research, *Design for Youth Development Policy,* p. 2.
15. Ibid., p. 36.
16. Coleman, *Youth: Transition to Adulthood,* p. 2.
17. Ibid., p. 87.
18. Lipsitz, *Growing Up Forgotten,* p. 17.
19. Ibid., p. 121.
20. National Commission on Excellence in Education, *A Nation at Risk: The Imperative for Educational Reform* (Washington, D. C.: U.S. Government Printing Office, 1983), p. 8.
21. Lipsitz, *Growing Up Forgotten,* p. 125.
22. Bureau of Education for the Handicapped, *Progress Toward a Free Appropriate Public Education* (Washington, D. C.: U.S. Department of Health, Education, and Welfare, 1979), p. 23.
23. Lipsitz, *Growing Up Forgotten,* pp. 136-43.
24. Ibid., p. 147

25. Bureau of Education for the Handicapped, *Progress Toward a Free Appropriate Public Education*, p. 23.
26. Lipsitz, *Growing Up Forgotten*, p. 184.
27. Ibid., p. 185.
28. Center for Action Research, *Design for Youth Development Policy*, p. 24.
29. Kakalik et al., *Services for Handicapped Youth*, p. 16.
30. Liptsitz, *Growing Up Forgotten*, p. 192.
31. *New York Times*, February 18, 1979, Sec. 4, p. E7.
32. Lipsitz, *Growing Up Forgotten*, p. 208.
33. Michael C. Dixon and William E. Wright, *Juvenile Delinquency Prevention Programs* (Nashville, Tenn.: Institute on Youth and Social Development, John F. Kennedy Center for Research on Education and Human Development, George Peabody College for Teachers, October 1974), p. 11.
34. Social Research Group, *Toward Interagency Coordination: An Overview of Federal Research and Development Activities Relating to Adolescence*, First Annual Report (Washington, D.C.: George Washington University, 1973), p. 28.
35. Lipsitz, *Growing Up Forgotten*, p. 157.
36. John P. Hill, "Some Perspectives on Adolescence in American Society" (Position paper prepared for the Office of Child Development, U.S. Department of Health, Education, and Welfare, Washington, D.C., May 1973), mimeographed, p. 88.
37. Ibid., pp. 182–87.
38. Sebald, *Adolescence: A Social Psychological Analysis*, p. 4.
39. Lipsitz, *Growing Up Forgotten*, p. 154.
40. Allan G. Green, "Planning for Declining Enrollments," *School Review* 82 (August 1974): 597.
41. Center for Action Research, *Design for Youth Development Policy*, pp. 30-31.
42. Coleman, *Youth: Transition to Adulthood*, p. 146.
43. Ibid., pp. 145-72.
44. *U.S. Code Annotated*, Section 3811.
45. Ibid., Section 5671.
46. Lipsitz, *Growing Up Forgotten*, p. 174.
47. President's Council on Youth Opportunity, *Youth Resources Manual* (Washington, D.C.: U.S. Government Printing Office, March 1971).
48. Gisela Konopka, *Young Girls: A Portrait of Adolescence* (Englewood Cliffs, N.J.: Prentice-Hall, 1976), cited in Lipsitz, *Growing Up Forgotten*, p. 181.
49. For an interesting treatment and more detailed explication of the suggested competencies, see Betty L. Baer and Ronald Federico, *Educating the Baccalaureate Social Worker* (Cambridge, Mass.: Ballinger Publishing Co., 1978).

Human Resource Development in Organizations

Leonard Nadler

DEFINING THE FIELD

The nature of learning experiences for adults in nonschool settings has been and will continue to be difficult to describe. The form of these experiences varies and constantly changes in relation to society and the wide range of people who are being served. This chapter will focus on those learning experiences provided for employees and nonemployees by various types of organizations—business and industry, government, labor organizations, and voluntary organizations.

Brief History

Nonschool education provided by organizations has been known by many names, and, therefore, a strict historical treatment is almost impossible. For many years, the most common term used to describe such education has been *training*. The first training program, it has been suggested, took place when a tribe (a form of organization) evolved a system to teach its young people how to care for animals or how to make weapons. As time passed, more and more examples of "training" emerged, although in many cases these would be instances of what we today call "on-the-job training." Typically, this involved a person being placed in a position requiring performance; if the person could not perform, older (and presumably wiser) members of the organization had the responsibility for instructing the younger member. Documented experiences of such learning activities are few, but they do exist; however, to date, nobody has written a history. Such a study would have to emphasize the preparation of leaders for organizations such as the government and the military, and in the economic arena, the practices of the guilds.

In more recent times, the Industrial Revolution brought about the need for more formalized instruction because relying on learning by trial and error proved too costly when machinery was involved. Slowly, employing organizations began to provide purposeful instruction to employees prior to their operating machinery. In the latter part of the 1800s, such instruction took place in factories themselves.

For the United States, as for a number of other industrial countries, the major impetus for industrial training came during World War I where demands required a speedy growth of the industrial complex. Workers were rapidly placed in situations in which prior experience could not be an effective teacher. The work of Dr. Charles Allen of the Federal Board for Vocational Education was significant in creating such programs called Training Within Industry (TWI); these programs were continued after the war, but at such a decreased level that they seemed to have disappeared. With the advent of World War II, the programs were revived; even today there are those who believe the TWI program began with this second conflict, though its origin in World War I is clear. While it is unfortunate that employing organizations needed an international crisis to recognize the worth of educating their employees, World War II nevertheless provided an impetus that is still with us and appears to be growing.

Programs implemented in the 1960s for the disadvantaged further accelerated the growth of nonschool education for adults. The Manpower Development Act of 1962, the Economic Opportunity Act of 1964, and similar legislation emphasized learning as a way of improving the economic and social position of the disadvantaged.

Human Resource Development

Some of the confusion in the field is due to the lack of agreed-upon terminology. For this chapter, as has been the case in other discussions of the issue, the author proposes the term *human resource development* (HRD) to encompass the learning experiences under consideration.

HRD is the organized learning experience provided by an organization with the intent of bringing about possible behavioral change. "Learning experience" is the crucial phrase. There are any number of ways to help people grow, but HRD is directly concerned with learning. "Organized" is also essential. There is always the possibility that an individual may learn from nonorganized opportunities, but HRD deals with those experiences that are organized. These may be formal (that is, take place in a classroom) or informal (that is, occur by means of on-the-job coaching), but in either case they are organized learning activities, with defined learning objectives, a specified time to accomplish the learning, and some form of evaluation. It is also important to understand the phrase "possible behavioral change." The first of its two components is "behavioral change." The learning is directed to a specific purpose, usually centrally related to the goals of the organization. The second element, that change is only "possible," is important, as learning *may* lead to behavioral change, but this cannot be guaranteed. The individual may learn the new behavior but then be prevented from using it because of factors outside the scope of the HRD field. This limitation has given rise to a companion field, *organizational development* (OD), but that field is even more ambiguous than HRD, and its range of definitions defies imagination. The focus of one aspect of OD is on bringing about congruency between the learned behavior and an increased opportunity actually to use that new behavior within the organization. In essence, HRD is a subset of OD.

It is possible to be more specific about HRD by examining the three types of learning experience—training, education, development—encompassed by that term. As organizations have begun to use this typology, they have found it possible to clarify the purpose of the learning for the benefit of both the individual learner and the organization. There is no hierarchical logic in the order of listing of the three types. HRD provides learning experiences for individuals irrespective of their status in the organization. All members of an organization may benefit from the three forms of HRD, as appropriate to needs.

1. *Training.* This consists of learning experiences designed to improve performance on a job presently held by the learner. The intent is that the employee use the learning upon returning to the job or while on the job as learning takes place. Training may become necessary for a number of reasons. For example, it may be required because new processes or materials are introduced into a job situation. A change of regulations can also trigger the need for training. Or the present job may be redesigned (for example, job enrichment, job enlargement), necessitating appropriate training on the present, though altered, job. Finally, the learner may have lost some skill over a period of time and needs training to regain the original skill level.

2. *Education.* This involves learning experience designed to prepare a person for a future defined job. The intent is not to use the learning on the present job but to enable the individual to move into a new job, usually because of a promotion. In times of economic recession, personnel may need education upon receiving a lateral transfer or even a demotion; usually, however, education prepares personnel for some kind of advancement.

3. *Development.* This consists of learning experiences designed for the distant future. There is no intent that the learning will be used on the present job or as preparation for a defined job in the near future. Rather, organizations provide development so that members of their work force can be kept alert to the directions of society, the organization, and individuals. These learning experiences may also be just for the general growth of the employee, though the Internal Revenue Service frowns upon this as a legitimate expense of an employing organization.

Settings

HRD takes place in a variety of settings, although there is little solid information about these settings, despite attempts by the Department of Labor and other agencies to gather such data. One reason for the lack of information is the previously noted lack of agreement on terminology. Another is that some private organizations prefer not to divulge the extent of their activity in the field. Actually, many organizations themselves do not know the extent of their involvement in HRD. Nationally, cost estimates run from $2 billion to $45 billion or more, depending on what activities are being included.

Although it is not always possible to list specific activities, we can identify the kinds of organizations that undertake HRD programs.

1. *Business and Industry.* By far, the greatest activity in HRD occurs in the private sector, that is, in business and industry. Some studies have indicated that firms with fewer than 500 employees typically tend not to have a formal HRD program. This is a problem, for such firms need this activity in order to compete successfully. Smaller firms frequently cope with this problem by hiring personnel who have benefited from HRD programs when employed by larger organizations.

   Within business and industry, some categories of firms are more likely than others to employ HRD. Some organizations are labor-intensive, that is, they rely more on people than on machinery. It might be expected that such labor-intensive organizations have greater HRD activity, although this is not necessarily so. Hospitals, for example, have been labor-intensive and will remain so; yet up until recently, hospitals did not provide HRD for all employees but, instead, focused their efforts essentially on nursing staff. The trend now is to expand HRD opportunities to other categories of hospital personnel.

2. *Government.* In the federal government, HRD activity is commonly known as "training and development" and is authorized by the Government Employees Training Act of 1958, as amended. The federal government designates Employee Development Specialists—some 26,000 of them—to undertake HRD activity, but there are many other persons involved in HRD functions who carry other titles. The upper limit is probably far in excess of the official number.

   At the state and local levels there is also activity in HRD, although not nearly as well defined or funded as at the federal level. To help bridge this gap, the Intergovernmental Personnel Act supports state and local HRD efforts by arranging for exchanges of qualified HRD personnel among various governmental units at all levels.

3. *Labor Unions.* Traditionally, labor unions provided HRD programs in the form of apprenticeships and on topics related to the operation of labor unions. More recently, the Human Resource Development Institute of the AFL-CIO, located in Silver Spring, Maryland, has been created to provide training and education for labor leaders and potential labor leaders. Individual unions have their own programs, some of which date back several decades.

It is likely that unions will become more involved in other forms of HRD. One force stimulating this change is "industrial democracy," wherein labor and management share responsibilities for planning and management. This movement, prevalent in Western Europe, is showing signs of emerging in the United States. It takes many forms, but in some of these, union members need to know much more about management, finance, and other traditional areas that have typically been outside of the range of union-sponsored HRD programs.

4. *Voluntary Organizations.* The United States, which has the reputation of being a "nation of joiners," probably has more voluntary organizations, as related to the size of population, than any other country. Some of these organizations are small and local, such as civic associations. At the other end of the spectrum are such national organizations as the American Red Cross, the American Cancer Society, the YMCA and YWCA, and the Rotarians. By no means is this list indicative of the range of organizations. There are about 20,000 different recognized voluntary associations in the United States. Not all of them have HRD programs, but many do.

GOALS OF HUMAN RESOURCE DEVELOPMENT

The Learner

The goals of HRD activity must first be related to the types of learners, HRD's two major constituencies: employees and nonemployees.

1. Employees are easy to identify. They are those persons who are on the payroll of an organization, usually, though not always, as regular full-time employees. These employees may be scattered at

a variety of sites and may be doing a wide range of jobs. They may encompass several shifts or varying hours of employment. Because the jobs of employees are usually specific, it is not too difficult to apply the HRD typology in order to identify the kinds of learning programs provided by an employer. Most programs will be in the training and education categories. Organizations that also provide development are usually among the more stable and high-risk organizations. They can afford this kind of investment, which has no guarantee of immediate return for the organization.

2. Nonemployees are more difficult to identify, though by no means are they few in number. To reach its goals, an organization may have to provide a great deal of HRD to persons who are not employees, most obviously in such areas as customer training and education. HRD personnel encourage consumers to purchase and use a product, and they range from the salesperson who demonstrates (and teaches) how to use a cosmetic line sold by the organization, to the computer service representative who instructs employees of a purchaser on how to use the equipment.

Government HRD programs for nonemployees are quite extensive. The Internal Revenue Service, for example, provides learning resources on aspects of preparing income tax returns. The Job Corps program services nonemployees because workers are assigned to the program only temporarily and thus are not considered government employees. The Agricultural Extension Service provides an example of an extremely large personnel group that is usually not considered to be involved in HRD functions; actually, however, staff serve a working population (usually rural) in order to help improve the condition of agricultural work and life. Such activity can be considered HRD for nonemployees.

The Organization

When they see a purpose, organizations utilize their financial and physical resources to develop their human resources. Most frequently, the purpose is related to the economic goals of the organization, but there has been increasing interest in the social goals of the community in which the organization exists. One often hears, however, about the "bottom line." For the most part, if employee HRD does not contribute to the profit picture of the organization, why undertake it? If a business or industry does not make a profit, it does not survive. Therefore, there is a strong economic orientation to most HRD programs in business and industry.

However, once an organization has achieved economic stability, other goals may emerge, and these may be served by HRD. Large, well-established organizations often have HRD programs for non-employees as well as for employees, directed toward improving some non-job-related behaviors. These are usually not too well advertised or documented for a very basic economic reason. Company officials are reluctant to be forced to defend expenditures for HRD that do not contribute to the bottom line of profitability. Stockholders can become quite irate when they discover that the company has used its resources for some activity not contributing to profit and dividends. Even the Internal Revenue Service takes a dim view of expenditures that are not directly related to the business.

The orientation to profit and economic factors may be the single most difficult problem faced by professional educators who seek to leave schools and colleges and venture into world of HRD. Altruism may still be present, but performance is frequently evaluated in different terms. There is no longer the question of how many passed, how many did not drop out, how many received scholarships, and so forth. The question that faces the professional educator working in HRD areas in the private sector is, how did your activity contribute to the goals—particularly, the economic goals—of the organization?

PRESENT OPPORTUNITIES

There are opportunities available to professional educators who wish to move into HRD. The number of jobs available varies, of course, depending upon the state of the economy and the prevailing attitude toward human resources. The major variables that influence job opportunities are competencies and company policy.

Roles

Competencies of the HRD person are best identified through role behaviors. There has been considerable research for over twenty years on the roles of HRD personnel in business, industry, government, and voluntary organizations. There has been much less research conducted on HRD in the labor field, but it is likely that the typology of roles outlined below would still prevail.

Learning Specialists. This is the most obvious role and perhaps the one with which professional educators most easily identify. Although it is not the role most frequently valued by organizations, the professional educator who wishes to move from the school to another setting can readily serve in this role and thereby gain entry into a new field.

The learning specialist contains three subroles. The facilitator of learning acts as a teacher; although in organizational settings there are many more possibilities than just traditional classroom instruction. All of the usual teacher competencies are useful in this subrole, although a significant dimension of the role is that the learning facilitator is primarily concerned with teaching adults, not children. The importance of this dimension cannot be overstated.

Another subrole is a designer of learning programs. This role involves more than just the development of curriculum, although competencies related to curriculum building are certainly useful here. The learning programs called for generally relate to the world of work, and too few professionals from schools of education have been prepared to function in this milieu. For one thing, many individuals and groups must be involved in the design process, and, for another, there is usually a short time span for delivering the completed product, the learning program. The focus of a learning program generally is job performance, and the designer of learning programs must be able to plan and conduct immediate evaluation of behavioral change.

The learning program may also have to be designed to be conducted by a facilitator of learning who is not a professional in the field of learning. This places the curriculum designer under constraints not usually present in a typical school situation. However, this offers an interesting challenge and encourages a creativity in planning that the designer may find refreshing.

A third subrole of a learning specialist is as instructional strategies developer. The term *instructional strategies* is used to embrace all teaching approaches usually suggested by techniques, methods, devices, and formats. This list is by no means exhaustive, and the search for definitions of these terms can be exhausting. Rather than utilize valuable time to distinguish among these terms, the tendency has been to include them all as various kinds of instructional and learning strategies. It is possible that at some future date an agreement on terms will emerge, but we are not yet able to discern such agreement. The professional who moves from the school to the private sector must avoid becoming involved in jurisdictional disputes over terminology, but, rather, continue to explore the wide range of strategies available to support the designer and enhance the work of the facilitator—all toward helping the learner.

To reiterate an earlier point, all those involved as learning specialists must recognize that their students are adults. Unless this is fully recognized and appropriate accommodations made, failure is inevitable. Although there are still some who hold that an adult is just a grown child, the practitioner will find that such an approach is completely unacceptable in the field of HRD in nonschool settings. Adults differ greatly in terms of age, experience, background, current role in society, motivation, and expectations, and all these differences have great impact on the kind of learning situations to be designed and conducted.

Administrator. The administrator of nonschool learning situations will find that the problems of administration closely mirror those found by almost any other administrator in an organizational setting. There are four major areas of activity (or subroles): developer of HRD personnel, supervisor of programs, maintainer of relations, and arranger of facilities and finance. These subroles are not unique to the HRD field, but some of the terminology and goals discussed below will indicate differences.

The developer of HRD personnel works mainly with full-time HRD personnel, and this is not too much different from the situation in school settings. In addition, however, the developer works with part-time and temporary HRD people, some of whom may come from outside the organization, while others may be employed in other units of the organization and have been assigned some HRD duties.

School personnel may not always be familiar with utilizing part-time personnel, even though in recent years the use of external consultants appears similar in both school and nonschool settings. The difference may be in the extent of such use—part-time personnel are used much more frequently in nonschool settings.

The use of temporary HRD people is quite common when units within the organization have personnel with particular competencies required for part of a HRD program. These temporary people might join the HRD unit for a specified period of time as subject matter specialists to assist in designing learning programs and even to undertake some of the instruction.

The supervisor of programs may be compared in certain ways with a principal or other supervisor in a school setting. The role involves applying the principles and practices of planning, control, coordination, and so forth. Outside the schools, programs do not start and stop on a regular basis, but there are important differences—semesters are comparatively unknown. Even times of the workday will vary greatly depending upon work shifts or the physical location of the learners. The expectations of the organization are also different. Annual reports may still be required, but the supervisor is also expected to provide feedback to management and line units upon the completion of a learning program.

The role of maintainer of relations will be familiar to any school person who has had to give speeches, respond to phone calls, and generally be available to the public, parents, government officials, and learners. The questions posed may be different, but the process is the same. In this subrole, the school educator may even bring to the situation some understandings that currently appear to be lacking in the private sector.

Likewise, as an arranger of facilities and finance the school person usually has had some experience that may prove helpful. But the school person is cautioned not to try to build a schoolhouse or even schoolrooms. Facilities in the private sector cover a wider range of possibilities. Some organizations have residential learning centers that appear to duplicate higher education institutions. In these centers, educators are likely to find that their prior experience is helpful. In organizations that emphasize decentralized or individual learning facilities, it may be necessary to explore new avenues in arranging for facilities.

Consultant. In HRD, the practice of consulting is growing rapidly and provides many opportunities. Despite this, little will be said about it here. The role of consultant has so many variations that a description is impossible in the limited space available. Teachers are likely to have used consultants in the past and perhaps have even functioned as consultants themselves. An overview of the field, with models and experiences, can be found in many books. The important point to consider is that consulting is a process—a way of providing a service. What one consults about can vary from building bridges to settling an international crisis. A consulting relationship attempts to match the expertise of a consultant with the need of a client in a particular situation.

Some organizations employ regular full-time consultants, who are referred to as internal consultants. Some of these will be found in the activity known as organization development (OD), a field which has its roots in organizational behavior rather than in learning. A person who wishes to be a consultant in OD is advised to obtain a background in organizational behavior and in the theories of organizations.

There are also external consultants who move from organization to organization for varying periods of time. This is a high-risk position for the consultant, for it depends on contracts and payments, both of which may have nothing to do with the competence of the consultant. There is a great deal of competition in the field among external consultants, and there is a constant turnover. There are consultants who have been in the field for quite a while and are still operating successfully. Becoming an external consultant is a high-risk venture that requires sufficient capital to endure the uneven flow of contracts and the protracted method of payment resulting from the indeterminate length of a consulting contract.

The Setting Within an Organization

It should be obvious from the above that there is much that the school person can bring into the nonschool setting. A major problem is encountering differences in the new setting once one joins an organization.

Placement in the Organization.   School personnel are accustomed to working in institutions whose primary endeavor is providing learning for students. This is not the major objective in business, industry, government, labor unions, and voluntary organizations. In each of these, learning is only one small part of the total operation of the organization.

HRD activities are performed in many parts of the organization. At one time those activities could be found in the personnel department. This still exists in some organizations, but the trend is for HRD to be set up as a separate unit.

Where HRD is found in personnel, the school person must explore the situation. It could mean that the only advancement within the organization is into personnel positions, such as recruitment, compensation, and appraisal. Where HRD exists as a unit separate from personnel, the possibility exists of moving up within the HRD function and making direct use of what the school person knows about learning.

An alternative, of course, is for the school person to use HRD as a way of entering the private sector. From the HRD position it may be possible to move in many different directions within organizations, if that is the career pattern being sought.

Cosmopolitans and Locals. Research by some sociologists indicates that some professionals (that is, cosmopolitans) look to their field for leadership and direction, while others (that is, locals) look to their current employer. This means that the HRD function can be staffed by persons who view their work in HRD as a temporary assignment by their company. These latter persons feel they will be in a HRD position for only a short period of their work life with the company and are constantly looking for that next assignment, probably outside the HRD area.

For school people this can prove very disconcerting, for they may be accustomed to working with colleagues who view schools and learning as a career. Certainly, there is movement in and out of the school field, but essentially there is a large core of those who spend their lives in the field of learning. The school person may find that is not the situation in a private sector organization. In some organizations, HRD personnel may even be looked upon with suspicion because their loyalties may lie with a professional field, not with the employing organization. There are no easy answers to this dilemma. Although the problem is pervasive, it has not been particularly acute until recently as more people come to identify themselves with their professions rather than their employers.

PROFESSIONAL PREPARATION

There is no one specific academic preparation for people who want to enter the HRD field. A review of the positions available in any of a number of publications indicates that employers are seeking a wide range of professional backgrounds, some of them almost unrelated to the work. This is a reflection of the state of the field; employers are still not sure of just whom they want to hire to provide learning experiences for employees.

HRD work requires no certification, licensure, or accreditation, though there have been some feeble attempts to implement these measures. As with related forms of adult education that are not school based, the question arises as to who wants certification and for what purpose? At present, the consumer (that is, employer) is not asking for this, and it is doubtful if there will emerge any strong movement in this direction. Some HRD-related membership organizations are exploring efforts toward certification or accreditation, but this is mainly to serve the needs of members, not employers.

People enter the HRD field from many disciplines. There are several reasons for this. For example, many people do not discover the field until after they have completed an undergraduate and, in some cases, a master's program. Courses related to HRD are available in many institutions of higher education. These learning experiences will be found in the numerous institutions that offer graduate programs in adult education.

The professional preparation of an individual entering the HRD field should be related to professional goals. If the person wants to adopt HRD as a profession, then a degree in HRD—in Adult Education—would be appropriate. If the individual is a "local" as described earlier, then a degree in HRD or adult education would be restrictive.

In addition to the academic work described above, numerous seminars and workshops are available. Several listings of these opportunities are available monthly, quarterly, or annually. There are no criteria as yet to indicate which of these are more desirable than others; it is a good idea to follow the rule of caveat emptor concerning these offerings. Nonacademic experiences provide not only learning, of course, but also direct contact with others in the field. This can be helpful for professional mobility.

FUTURE OPPORTUNITIES

It is risky to write of future opportunities in a field that still lacks adequate definition. All indications suggest that the field is growing as more attention is being given to human resources. Three factors will influence the future: (1) organization policies, (2) the economy, and (3) federal policies.

Organization Policies

During the 1950s the most prevalent HRD programs involved the area of human relations. With the advent of the 1960s and a new emphasis on technology, the thrust was more toward finding technical solutions to problems, with less emphasis on people. The history of the 1960s has given adequate testimony to the fallacy of that approach.

The increased use of technology has changed the work place. At first, this may have seemed dehumanizing, but we are now moving in the direction of increasing our attention on people as part of organizations. HRD is, of course, only one part of the total picture related to human resources, but it is the part we are concerned with here.

It may be a while before some organizations move fully in this direction, but the larger organizations, as usual, will take the lead. We can expect to find more policy statements related to HRD, making HRD offerings more available than is now the case. Alternative life-styles, flexi-time, job-sharing, and similar practices will increase the need for well-organized and appropriately staffed HRD units.

The Economy

Despite the desire to move in the direction of increased attention to human resources, the economy is always a countervailing force. At this time in the United States, many factors are in conflict. Increased attention to human resources is being curtailed by persistent unemployment, that is, unemployment involving persons who want to work but cannot find jobs. Perhaps, given the contribution of technology, we will never have sufficient jobs for all who want to work. Other ways will have to be found to provide financial resources to support learning programs.

Some have suggested that when the economy suffers, training goes up! This is true if training is defined along the lines suggested earlier in this chapter. The emphasis of this definition is on higher productivity and a more efficient work force—both resulting from effective training programs. Education, as earlier defined, decreases, due to the lack of opportunities for movement. Development almost disappears. The work of HRD goes on, but in a much different fashion as it responds to changes in the economy.

Federal Policies

The role of the federal government in HRD has been limited. True, the Senate Committee on Labor and Manpower changed its name to the Committee on Human Resources. Programs for disadvantaged and minorities have received limited federal funding. Aside from these meager efforts and others less well known, there has been little leadership at the federal level. One can question whether there should be, but the evidence strongly suggests that Congress will be passing additional legislation regarding HRD. Although HRD is most extensive in the private sector, it is coming under the close scrutiny that Congress gives to all aspects of economic and social life.

CONCLUSION

It is difficult to write a conclusion to this chapter. Even as it is being written, the field is changing. Human resource development is gaining recognition, and this is for the good; but as with any successful endeavor, HRD is bringing in many who rally to the flag without knowing the cause. The confusion in the field is not likely to diminish in the years to come. The field can use many professionals in the field of learning who are prepared to work in nonschool settings.

PART III

Colleges of Education: New Opportunities

In this final chapter the editors argue that colleges of education should consider their mission for the future in two contexts. First, they contend that colleges of education within major universities should provide the leadership needed to upgrade the professional status of the colleges and of practitioners in the field of education. This can be done, they propose, if programs for the initial preparation and for the continuing education of educators are inquiry-based and are built upon a continuing search for new knowledge related to practice.

Second, they point to significant transformations currently taking place in the human service professions and note that much of the knowledge and many of the skills commonly taught in colleges of education have direct relevance to the educational tasks confronting the human service professions as a result of these transformations. They give examples of such knowledge and skills that would clearly be applicable to the human service professions generally. Finally, they suggest four possible approaches for colleges of education that choose to expand their mission to include a role in the human services. They believe that this broader mission would recognize that it is necessary for people of all ages to learn constantly in order to survive, participate effectively, and thrive in the society of today.

CHAPTER
10

Colleges of Education: The Profession, Human Services, and the Future

Charles W. Case and
William A. Matthes

Colleges of education in major teaching and research universities should consider their mission for the future in two contexts. The first is that of the role of the major universities in the development of the "professional" nature of the college of education beyond its current ambiguous status as something more than a normal school but not quite a professional school. The second context concerns relating education-based knowledge and skills to other human service practices in a variety of societal settings. Contrary to those who seek more limited and specialized missions for colleges of education, we argue for a broader, yet defined, mission, a mission that recognizes the necessity for all people of all ages to learn constantly in order to survive, participate effectively, and thrive.

THE DEVELOPMENT OF THE PROFESSION

Other authors in this volume have described the historical development of the preparation of educators. They have noted the development of normal schools and the establishment of schools or colleges of education in universities or the expansion of normal schools into regional universities. Some authors have noted that within academe, colleges of education have often been considered suspect. We contend that this state of affairs may be the result of six interrelated factors that continue to plague the "profession" of education and colleges of education.

From the earliest days of this country, teaching youngsters has been perceived by both teachers and citizens as an activity that is learned through a type of *apprenticeship preparation* (that is, if one indeed needed to *learn* how to teach youngsters at all). This apprenticeship mentality is still prevalent. The document from the National Education Association (NEA), *Excellence in Our Schools: Teacher Education*,[1] is replete with statements that assert that the preparation of future teachers should be based on what current, practicing teachers believe are the essential skills and knowledge necessary for successful practice and on extended periods of practice teaching. We would assert that such recommendations are clearly geared to training, not to the educational development of professionals who, as such, are capable of exercising judgment and adapting to changing conditions. Such training does not prepare professionals to be committed to constant inquiry about their practice, nor does it add to the profession new knowledge that may change and improve methods of practice. In addition, such an orientation to the preparation of teachers will not provide teachers or curriculums that prepare youngsters to live and change in a future that may be vastly different from the past or present. We have cited the recent NEA publication, but many other reports from a variety of professional associations and recent national commissions also err in the same direction. The belief in the apprentice model has pervaded policy and practice throughout the history of teacher education in the United States.

A second and related barrier to considering teaching a profession is the existence of *too many institutions of higher education sanctioned to prepare teachers*. This has been emphasized by other authors in this volume. Hendrik Gideonse, for example, has noted that other professions have historically encountered the same phenomenon. Medicine and law took control of their own professions, developed preparation programs based on the best knowledge available at the time, and instituted these programs in major universities. In this process they committed their professions to an inquiry-based epistemology, purposely breaking away from practice based on myth and supposition. They established a new belief system and corresponding standards of quality and in the process greatly decreased the number of institutions allowed to provide preparation programs.

A third barrier is the *ongoing warfare within the profession* that operates to fragment the cohesion necessary for its advancement. Teachers unite through their professional associations against the "enemy" of school administrators and school boards, who, in turn, organize professional organizations around their respective roles. Professional educators in higher education do likewise, as do personnel from state departments of public instruction. Further fragmentation occurs within each of these sectors as each further subdivides into smaller groups representing particular subject or interest areas, professional roles, or groupings based on levels of education or employment in different settings. There is not one voice for education as with the American Medical Association or the American Bar Association. If there were an enemy that sought to render our profession ineffective, that enemy would hope to cause a system such as the one we have described.

The first three factors flow into a fourth, the *lack of commitment to an inquiry-based profession*. N.L. Gage has made the case eloquently for a profession so conceived and for the necessary relationships between a scientific basis for teaching and the art of teaching:

> In medicine and engineering, where the scientific basis is unquestionable, the artistic elements also abound. In teaching, where the artistic elements are unquestionable, a scientific base can also be developed. These professions are not in themselves sciences; they merely have scientific bases. To practice medicine and engineering requires a knowledge of much science: concepts, or variables, and their interrelations in the form of strong or weak laws, generalizations, or trends. But using the science to achieve practical ends requires artistry—the artistry that enters into knowing when to follow the implications of the laws, generalizations, and trends, and, especially, when *not* to, and how to combine two or more laws or trends in solving a problem.[2]

This proposal provides a dynamic, as opposed to a static, state for a profession.

The remaining two factors relate specifically to colleges of education. The fifth factor concerns *the lack of definition in the relationship between colleges of education and colleges of liberal arts*. As characterized by others all too often, education faculties do not attempt to influence instruction in liberal arts in a way that would allow future teachers to have the opportunity to learn more about intrinsic differences in structure among separate disciplines and how to use those differences to aid teaching and learning. In addition, some faculty of liberal arts view instruction in areas of education as superfluous or trivial.

As is true in other areas, preparation in colleges of education build upon the foundations provided by the liberal arts. Colleges of education were made part of universities to achieve this relationship, as well as to have teacher preparation occur in an environment that values and practices scholarly inquiry. If major universities abandon the commitment to professional education, as some now are doing, the preparation of educational professionals will be relegated to regional universities, successors of the normal schools that have not distinguished themselves by their scholarship. We will be charged with being elitist for making such a statement. So be it. For decades, survey after survey regarding research productivity reinforces the impression that the bulk of educational research is produced by fewer than 100 colleges of education in universities. If education is to become a profession, the involvement of major universities with a commitment to the liberal arts and scholarship will be essential.

The sixth factor also relates specifically to colleges of education within major universities, a factor some authors in this volume have alluded to when they note that some professors of education express *difficulties in fulfilling expectations and norms that accompany teaching, research, and service functions.* It is curious that one seldom hears the same concern from colleagues in other professional schools. Possibly, faculty in medicine, dentistry, law and other professional areas have been able to provide a clearer definition of their responsibilities in the areas of teaching, research, and service. There is more experimentalism in, say, a college of medicine than in a school of education. Different teaching techniques and instructional methods are tried out and evaluated. Curriculum change is also more constant. The belief system in most other professional schools is propelled by a constant search for new knowledge that quickly finds its way into curriculum. Service efforts usually include teaching and learning experiences, as well as a deliberate research effort. The faculty of a college of education tend to view each of the three functions as separate. But how can others value our activity when we cannot clearly delineate our

mission and demonstrate the interrelationships among these functions? If we do not seem assured, how can others have assurance
about what we do?

Education is intimately related to the liberal arts, but this does not
preclude the preparation of educators in a professional college. Other
professions are also dependent on knowledge from areas beyond an
immediate domain. It is essential that each faculty member in a major
university, no matter the discipline, interrelates and fulfills the three
functions of teaching, research, and service. These functions are not
separate, but central to generating, testing, and teaching new knowledge and practice. This orientation is particularly germane for faculty
in professional schools. Major universities and the colleges of education within them must make realities of these potentialities. The
rightful demands for excellence at all levels of education require no
less.

THE RELATIONSHIP OF PROFESSIONAL EDUCATION TO OTHER HUMAN SERVICE ENDEAVORS

Education as a profession is not quite a reality yet. There are,
though, trends occurring that can make education a profession. Many
of the trends that involve the relationship between colleges of education and school systems have been discussed in Part I of this book.

The remainder of this chapter will focus on the relationship between colleges of education and other human service professions. This
relationship, too, can strengthen the professional status of colleges of
education and, indeed, the profession of teaching. It is proposed here
that some colleges of education play a legitimate and desirable role in
the preparation of a variety of human service professionals based on
the knowledge and skills endemic to the discipline of education and
the changing mission inherent in most human service professions.

Many colleges of education have long served persons whose goals
included working in a nonschool environment, but in roles for which
knowledge and skills provided by a college of education were appropriate. This has been particularly true of certain graduate-level
programs offered by colleges of education. Most often these programs
include a core curriculum appropriate to an overall area of study, for
example, counselor education. Other courses provide experience in a

related emphasis, such as agency counseling, rehabilitation counseling, substance-abuse counseling, or marriage and family counseling. The same phenomenon has existed in special education and instructional design and technology, and to a lesser extent in educational administration, higher education, and teacher education.

To date, social agencies and health care institutions have been the primary employers of graduates of these programs. To a lesser but growing extent, business and industry, labor unions, government, and the military are also employers of prepared educators.

Education is increasingly being recognized by a variety of professionals as an important function in the delivery of human services to the public. Concomitantly, professional educators are increasingly sought to provide expertise in teaching and learning in a variety of settings and institutions beyond schools. In some instances colleges of education have been deliberate in modifying their program to meet these opportunities; more often, they have simply drifted in these directions aided by student interest. In recent years, as noted by Sam Yarger, Sally Mertens, and Kenneth Howey in Chapter 5, some colleges of education have moved in these directions in an attempt to maintain enrollments. It is distressing in these instances to discover how little professors of education know about the new environments their programs are supposedly entering or how unaware they are of the literature and debate that has been underway for many years regarding a philosophy of human services practice and preparation.

We will return to this matter, but we first need to examine briefly the field of human services itself, its ideology, and the transition to prevention and education in its delivery. We need also to review examples of generic knowledge and skills commonly found in colleges of education and some of the major considerations colleges of education have to face with regard to their possible participation in the human services.

The human service professions are commonly defined as those professions whose primary purpose is to provide services to individuals or groups in an effort to relieve suffering or enhance a biological, social, or psychological state of being. Professions commonly included are medicine, social work, psychology, and allied health areas. Increasingly, it is becoming accepted that education, law, and human resource development are also included.

The Human Services Concept

Joan Chenault and Fran Burnford have summarized *the basic tenets of the ideology of the human services concept*, in which they include: (1) the systematic integration of services, (2) comprehensiveness and accessibility, (3) client troubles defined as problems-in-living, (4) the generic characteristics of helping activities, and (5) accountability of service providers to clients.[3]

The Systematic Integration of Services. This takes into account a long-term problem encountered when individuals receive multiple services from multiple sources but most often without any coordination among the services. It has not been uncommon for various services to be contradictory and, therefore, counterproductive. In addition, persons being served have not always been aware of what services could be obtained or how to access those services. This state of affairs has resulted from fragmented policy initiatives and from the creation of bureaucratic structures designed to implement separate initiatives. These directions have sometimes been the result of separate disciplinary or professional efforts that neither have recognized the contributions of other professionals nor have chosen to work in an interprofessional fashion.

Comprehensiveness and Accessibility. This tenet concerns building cooperative relationships among service providers as these relate to an individual through a common community system of diagnosis, referral, and the provision of integrated services. Harold Demone and Herbert Schulberg note:

> In recent years, emphasis has been upon building linkages between existing and planned organizations rather than seeking to incorporate all relevant services within a single agency. After determining the basic needs of a group and essential services for meeting them, a consortium of agencies divides the responsibilities according to their particular expertise—use of interface teams—and attempts to maximize the assets and minimize the deficits of contemporary community patterns.[4]

Client Troubles as Problems-in-Living. This tenet significantly changes the perception of difficulties as arising from inherent deficiencies of the individual. The attempt here is to consider the individual as a whole in relationship to his or her environment and, further, to modify the environment and to provide the individual with opportunities to make choices and become more self-reliant. In addition, a client's troubles are no longer defined according to narrow categorical labels that primarily reflect the expertise of specialists. The focus is on growth and development rather than on the treatment of a "disease."

The Generic Characteristics of Helping Activities. This recognizes the overlapping use of the same bodies of knowledge and skill among various helping professions and the blurring of professional roles. While distinct differences and emphases exist among the various helping professions, there are commonalities. Until recently, most professions have stressed their differences, using licensure, training, and status systems to emphasize them. Only in recent years have cooperative interprofessional teams been more common. Clearly, however, some professionals within each of the helping professions still maintain a commitment to the older ideology.

Accountability of Service Providers to Clients. This reflects the belief that the providers of services must be accountable to the users of the services as well as to the general public providing support for the services. Clients have rights, now reinforced by laws, to participate in the design and monitoring of human services.

To this list of five components of the human services ideology, we would add a sixth, which may possibly be a larger category, subsuming the other five—*empowerment of the individual.* The helping professions are in a transitional phase of working together, a phase that views their contributions as ones that will help individuals to rely less on systems that keep them dependent. There is a new emphasis on providing the individual with learning experiences, information, and the right to choose. These are the means of empowerment.

Transition

The transition to preventive and educational processes within the human services provides a primary reason for the increased involvement and employment of educators in other helping professions.

Whether one focuses on the goal of empowerment of individuals within society or on the prevention of illness, the helping professions have each adopted an educational function. In the shift from curative to preventive care, behavioral, attitudinal, and value changes on the part of a client are usually required. Slick brochures or sixty-second television spots do not usually accomplish such changes. Knowledge and skill in the area of human growth and development, behavioral change, and educational development are required. According to E.D. Pellegrino, health professionals are seldom prepared to provide three essentials in patient education—positive promotion about well-being, prevention of illness, and instruction in self-help—because "these are not genuinely integrated into the self-image and behavior of the health professions."[5] The next section on generic knowledge and skills will suggest some of the areas that professional educators can contribute to the other helping professions.

Areas of Generic Knowledge and Skills

Numerous statements exist detailing the knowledge and skills essential to function in the human services sector of society. In examining the literature of specific professions involved in human services it becomes apparent that there are many common or generic areas of knowledge and skills. Dugald Arbuckle demonstrated this point almost two decades ago when he reviewed statements in the literature pertaining to the functions of counselors, psychologists, and social workers. His review illustrated that these professions had more in common than they have differences.[6] The differences among human service specialists exist primarily because of the specific information with which they work or the setting.

The generic knowledge and skills essential to function as a professional in the human service sector cluster around the following four major dimensions, which are not necessarily discrete or independent of each other:

1. *Knowledge of individual development in the environmental context.* If a basic tenet of the human service concept is to empower a client to resolve issues, there is implied an educational process. The human service professional is an educator.[7] The subject matter that is taught is not academic in nature but deals with resolving "problems-in-living." Human service educators need to consider the developmental stages of the client within the context as they respond to the client. The problems of an adolescent male in a

security facility are usually different from those of a widow in a care facility. Certainly, there are common problems the adolescent and widow confront, but there are some real differences given the client's developmental stage and the context in which they exist. To function as an educator, knowledge of human development, learning theory, and motivation is necessary. These are topics commonly taught by faculties in colleges of education.

2. *Knowledge of self and the human condition.* The human service educator is expected to develop an awareness of personal experience and an understanding of the human condition. Human service educators need a clearly thought through set of principles and values to guide their behavior as activists or advocates.[8] This suggests that a preparation program needs to structure experiences in which the participants' values and thoughts are challenged, clarified, and integrated into a meaningful open behavior pattern. The effectiveness of a human service educator is not simply the application of a special set of skills or the possession of certain bits of information. The research of Arthur Combs and others suggests that effectiveness is directly related to the individual's perception of self and others.[9] The human service educator needs a commitment to engage in continuous self-examination and a willingness to understand the human condition. Many preparation programs within colleges of education stress this dimension through practicum experiences and simulations.

3. *Skills in the communication processes.* Skills in human relations and instructional design transcend the professional groups in the human service sector. These are viewed as basic to all human services educators. Colleges of education have a wealth of experience in the development and delivery of preparation programs designed to improve communication. Programs designed to develop specific human relations skills such as empathy, interviewing, confrontation, and group management have their origins in colleges of education. In addition, the design of instructional programs has been a basic element in the preparation of educators for decades. The development of human relations skills and instructional design are integral parts of most colleges of education.

4. *Skills and knowledge in the management and influencing of human systems.* The knowledge base for this generic cluster is drawn from different

academic disciplines such as economics, humanities, sociology, law, business, psychology, ethics, and political science, yet many of the specific skills such as evaluation, consultation, measurement, and administration are taught in colleges of education. Colleges of education have historically focused the application of these skills upon only one human service system, the schools.

The identified clusters of generic knowledge and skills common to human service professionals are most commonly taught by colleges of education at major universities. Increasingly, other human service preparation programs within universities have turned to colleges of education to develop these skills and knowledge in their students. Colleges of medicine and law have requested assistance in training their students in interviewing skills while departments of social work have drawn upon the expertise found in colleges of education in working with handicapped populations or group-process skills. The contribution of colleges of education to the development of these skills and knowledge bases among human service educators is now being recognized.

FOUR APPROPRIATE ROLES FOR COLLEGES OF EDUCATION

There are four possible roles that colleges of education can serve within the human services sector: the preparation of human service educators, the preparation of human service generalists, service to the preparation of specialists in other human service professions, and models for interprofessional education and practice. These roles are not mutually exclusive. Various combinations and mutations of them are possible depending upon local conditions, expertise, and mission.

Human Services Educator Role

While professional education focused the majority of its energies on schools, a world of learning grew in society beyond schools and colleges that is estimated to serve three or four times as many people as the schools and colleges. It is estimated that 46 million people are provided educational programs in agricultural extension, community organizations, business and industry, government, and other organizations.

The idea of the human services educator is not a new one. Barbara Burch described the emphasis on "new missions" for education in a paper presented to the Teacher Education Council of State Colleges and Universities:

> It appears that many of our teacher education graduates are already working in new mission areas. They have already found how to use their expertise and talents to get a variety of teaching and other education-related positions, for at a time when graduates in many fields are experiencing unemployment upon graduation, we at least have the small comfort that education graduates have a lower than average underemployment rate. That is to say that our graduates are working in occupations for which their credentials would seem to qualify them.[10]

The increasing demand for training, instruction, research, evaluation, curriculum design, and materials development in business, government, and community service is an opportunity for colleges of education to utilize much of their existing knowledge and skill in new settings. While other examples are possible, it is becoming more common to find such programs emerging in the area of instructional design and technology within colleges of education. For example, Indiana University and the University of Iowa provide graduate-level programs with the specific intent of preparing educators for business, industry, health care settings, and other nonschool settings. The graduates of these programs are readily employed in training and development, staff development, and other human resource development areas.

In these instances education faculty have built upon their knowledge and continuing research efforts in education generally and with specific applications to particular learners, settings, and goals. Therefore, while faculty members from education are knowledgeable about teaching, learning, and related matters, they must learn about different settings and adult learners. Obviously some modifications are needed in the curriculums of the colleges, and new relationships must be established with other professional colleges and human service agencies.

The Interdisciplinary Preparation of Human Service Generalists

A new class of helping professionals has arrived on the human service delivery scene: human service generalists. Generalists have been characterized as having the ability to identify and use wide-ranging resources and services to meet client needs and problems, as not being limited to one categorical service responsibility, and as having training in a broad range of helping skills. Human service generalists have emerged in response to

> an increasing tendency to conceptualize the variety of health and social welfare services in a new way which emphasizes . . . the generic quality of the helping actions of professional and nonprofessional caregivers despite a diversity of training titles . . . as well as societal recognition of the common denominator inherent in the varied problems presented by clients of helping agencies.[11]

It is possible to train professionals with a generic background in human services who can move from one area of practice to another and work across areas in positions that are defined by the needs of the client rather than traditional professional boundaries. Preparation programs for these "interdisciplinary travelers" requires an interdisciplinary approach—a departure from models that emphasize the compartmentalization of knowledge.

An interdisciplinary framework can be developed through cooperation of colleges of education and other academic and professional areas. Some colleges of education have implemented interdisciplinary programs that lead to a bachelor of science degree in human services. The intent of these programs is to prepare a human services graduate who at various times functions as helper, human rights activist, political ombudsman, stimulator of human potential, and organizer and coordinator of services for individuals and groups. Such interdisciplinary programs are typically designed by faculty from education, psychology, economics, health, recreation, physical education, and communications. Each course or experience is designed for the program and is not merely a smorgasbord of existing courses. The critical element in these programs resides in programs that are specifically designed to serve the philosophy and practice undergirding the role of the human service generalist with perspectives and contributions from relevant disciplines.

The major program example of this effort is the College for Human Services in New York City, which provides two-year, four-year, and graduate degrees specifically designed for human service generalists. An example of such a program in a preexisting university structure can be found at the University of Wisconsin at Oshkosh. The Human

Services Program (B.S.) there was designed and implemented by faculty from various areas within education and various social science disciplines in liberal arts, as well as professionals from human service agencies. This pattern seems to be more typical of the smaller, regional universities.

Colleges of Education Serve Specialists Prepared by Other Human Service Areas

Specialists are defined as those service providers who function as highly knowledgeable experts in well-defined specialities such as nursing, psychology, rehabilitation counseling, and criminology. Specialists have further been described as persons who (1) focus on services covering a single major program area or single group, (2) take a particularistic view of their enterprise and its environment, (3) concentrate on specific techniques of a particular service, and (4) generally do not take an organizational perspective.[12]

In the past, professional programs that prepared specialists often devoted most of the curriculum to perfecting technical knowledge and skills. The development of interpersonal skills is often left to chance. Colleges of education can play a role in preparing specialists for effective interpersonal communications with clients. The specialists are not only "treating" the problem itself; they are also helping clients and their families cope with the realities of their problem.

Closely related to this shift is the new and growing emphasis on prevention. Prevention is essentially an educational function or process. It involves instructing patients or clients in the acquisition of the "life skills" needed to ward off potential mental, physical, and emotional problems. This requires instructional programming, materials development, and information-disseminating skills and techniques.

A final role for colleges of education is in the area of professional preparation of specialists. Without question, specialties are best equipped to provide the theoretical and practical knowledge and skill bases undergirding the professional program. However, colleges of education can assist in the arrangement of content and its delivery format. That is, pedagogical techniques are needed that can present specialized content in a multidisciplinary way and that relate directly to client problems. Educational design specialists are needed to collaborate on and design instructional programs and curricular formats that stress general approaches to problems and problem-solving.

Within and among the human service professions a redirection is needed and is slowly occurring to stress the generalizability and transferability of previously acquired specialized knowledge and skills. If, for example, professionals in medicine and social services truly desire to alter their practice to stress preventative approaches and practice, they will need to know about learning processes and skills in teaching, program development, and counseling. They cannot, as they do now, rely almost exclusively on media techniques or brochures to disseminate information and assume that the dissemination of information alone produces learning or behavioral change.

The possible contributions of colleges of education to other professional colleges described in this role are typical of the major research universities. It is common to find the joint appointment of faculty members from colleges of education with colleges of medicine, nursing, dentistry, business administration, public health, pharmacy, and law. This tends to be the case in both major public and private universities. In some instances (for example, in a college of medicine), a person with degrees in education will be employed full time to provide these services.

Interprofessional Education and Practice

The fourth role is characterized by a formal structure for the interdisciplinary examination of problems and opportunities for change in the human services that affect interprofessional concerns and the delivery of services.

Ohio State University has the most developed example of this role in its Commission on Interprofessional Education and Practice. The Commission draws on the research, methods, and knowledge of allied medicine, education, law, medicine, nursing, psychology, social work, and theology. Professionals representing these disciplines on the Commission come from the various professional colleges of Ohio State University, other academic institutions, and professional associations.

The Commission has three major goals: (1) to address problems that require interprofessional delivery of services, (2) to respond to changing social perspectives that bear on complex ethical issues that affect professionals, and (3) to respond to changing relationships between consumers and professionals. The Commission uses three primary methods to achieve its goals: graduate and continuing education courses designed for interprofessional communication and practice, continuing education conferences for professionals working in the areas of human service need, and dissemination of information related to interprofessional education and practice.

SUMMARY

For colleges of education that expand their mission to include one or more of the suggested roles in the human services, there are a number of serious considerations to examine. Often the first issue encountered is the tension between generalization and specialization. This is particularly true if the goal is to establish a program to prepare human service generalists, which is often viewed as infringing upon the turf of social workers. The issue of generalization versus specialization is less severe and, on some campuses, almost nonexistent when colleges of education move toward one or more of the other three roles described in this chapter.

The critical elements for colleges of education attempting to move more deliberately into the human services are information and collaboration. The education faculty members who become involved must be informed about the issues, beliefs, and practices in the particular human service professions with which they wish to work. They must be willing to participate in cooperative projects wherein they will apply their expertise to settings and roles that may be new to them. Educators do bring to the task knowledge and skills that are valued by many professionals, as well as extensive experience in working with practitioners.

Interdisciplinary cooperation on campus varies greatly from institution to institution. On some campuses faculty members who are on joint appointments between two disciplines experience a lack of support in personnel decisions; on other campuses this is not an issue. Campus history and culture will be a major determinant in choosing which of the four human service roles is possible.

In terms of organizational structure many options are possible depending upon the role sought and local conditions. Some campuses achieve interdisciplinary programs through new independent institutes or similar arrangements; others achieve cooperation through shared goals and shared faculty members in a shared governance system across colleges and departments. The key elements are that the goal is shared, the activity is a priority among the participating colleges, and the participating colleges commit resources to achieve the goal.

The expansion of mission of some colleges of education to include a role in the preparation and practice of other human service professionals or to prepare educators to enter into human service organizations should not be an abandonment of its mission to serve the nation's schools. Rather such an expanded mission for qualified colleges of education can enhance the school mission through its involvement and credibility with other professionals who also serve children and their families. The expanded mission also can serve the many educational functions that continue to enlarge in the human service professions.

Colleges of education at major teaching and research universities must give the profession new form based upon research. This form need not be restricted to the preparation of educators just for schools but could easily include human service settings. However, whatever the form, careful consideration must be given to the future. The interdependence of institutions and individuals needs to be recognized as we move into a new era. To ignore the future, given present trends, would be irresponsible. Education will help shape the future, and colleges of education need to create a sense of the future among educators.

NOTES

1. National Education Association, *Excellence in Our Schools: Teacher Education* (Washington, D.C., 1982).
2. N. L. Gage, *The Scientific Basis of the Art of Teaching* (New York: Teachers College Press, 1978), p. 18.
3. Joan Chenault and Fran Burnford, *Human Services Professional Education: Future Directions* (New York: McGraw-Hill, 1978).
4. Harold W. Demone, Jr., and Herbert C. Schulberg, "Human Services Trends in the Mid-1970s," *Social Casework* 56 (May 1975): 278.
5. E.D. Pellegrino, "An Attitude and Method in Interprofessional Education," in *A Flexible Design for Health Professions Education*, edited by R. M. Jacobs (New York: Wiley, 1976), pp.203-4.
6. Dugald S. Arbuckle, "Counselor, Social Worker, Psychologist: Let's Ecumenicalize," *Personnel and Guidance Journal* 45 (February 1967): 532-38.
7. See Robert J. Nash and Edward R. Ducharme, "A Futures Perspective on

Preparing Educators for the Human Service Society: How to Restore a Sense of Social Purpose to Teacher Education," *Teachers College Record* 77 (May 1976): 444-71.

8. See Aubrey C. Cohen, "The Founding of a New Profession: The Human Service Professional" (Unpublished manuscript, New York City College for Human Services, 1974): Joseph Mehr, *Human Services: Concepts and Intervention Strategies* (Boston: Allyn & Bacon, 1980), p. 26; Nash and Ducharme, "Futures Perspective on Preparing Educators for the Human Service Society," p. 449; Eveline D. Schulman, *Intervention in Human Services* (St. Louis, Mo.: C. V. Mosby and Co., 1974).

9. Arthur W. Combs et al., *Florida Studies in the Helping Professions, University of Florida Social Science Monograph*, no. 37 (Gainesville: University of Florida Press, 1969).

10. Barbara Burch, "New Missions for Colleges of Education" (Paper presented to the Teacher Education Council of State Colleges and Universities, Nashville, Tenn., October 1979), p. 5.

11. Frank Baker, "From Community Mental Health to Human Services Ideology," *American Journal of Public Health* 64 (June 1974): 576-81.

12. Mark Yessian and Anthony Broskowski, "Generalities in Human-Service Systems: Their Problems and Prospects," *Social Service Review* 51 (June 1977): 265-88.